GARDENING
FOR
GOURMETS

*Good Eating from
a Small Back Yard*

Books by Ruth A. Matson

The Questing Cook
Cooking by the Garden Calendar
Gardening for Gourmets

GARDENING
FOR
GOURMETS

*Good Eating from
a Small Back Yard*

RUTH A. MATSON

Drawings by Margot Tomes

AN AMERICAN GARDEN GUILD BOOK

Doubleday & Company, Inc., Garden City, New York 1959

ACKNOWLEDGEMENTS

I take pleasure in thanking friends and fellow gardeners who over the years have encouraged my adventures in gardening for good eating. I wish especially to thank the staff of the Cleveland Garden Center for information and wise advice on many fine points of horticulture.

For this book, as my experience has widened, I have rewritten and elaborated upon some of the ideas originally presented in my series, "The Companionable Arts," which appeared in *Gourmet Magazine* in 1957, and have developed other ideas touched upon in articles written for the magazines, *The Flower Grower, The Home Garden,* and *House & Garden.* Thus GARDENING FOR GOURMETS brings up to date the personal history of my back-yard vegetable garden.

CONTENTS

Contents

Contents

GARDENING

FOR

GOURMETS

*Good Eating from
a Small Back Yard*

I

DREAM

OF

A GARDEN

The best way to plan a garden, as I rediscover every spring, is to settle comfortably in an armchair before dinner and dream about food. For there is a natural affinity between gardening and the supreme enjoyment of good eating. Some gardeners there are, to be sure, whose interest stops short at the kitchen door, whose creative impulses are fulfilled by the raising of prolific crops or mammoth specimens worthy of horticultural prizes. Fair enough, but this book is not for them. This book is a record of one back-yard garden, written for the gardener whose imagination is caught by the prospect of vegetables and salads at peak of succulence, to be enjoyed at once at the supper table. We have only to think of stepping to the garden to cut asparagus while the ingredients of hollandaise await within, to grasp what satisfactions this approach to gardening can offer.

Years of hearty good appetite led me to gardening. I was as aware as any connoisseur of the importance of youth and freshness in vegetables, fruits, and herbs; I used to market patiently for young peas, fresh-picked corn, and the like. I cultivated the generosity of gardening friends. In short, I accepted the dependence of good eating on good gardening, but it never occurred to me to have a vegetable patch of my own. That, I thought from the talk of gardening friends, was a major undertaking and only for the initiate.

My first awakening came in Italy, when Gino, the local florist, brought from his family garden the first cutting of broccoli— broccoli such as I had never seen in any market, tight little pointed heads as closely packed as cauliflower, cupped in dark green leaves. Cook it ten minutes only, he warned me strictly, and use no dressing but salt and pepper, oil and a little lemon juice. Oh yes, of course the *parmigiano*. I found my mouth watering, not in anticipation of the feast in store, but at the idea of someday growing my own broccoli to cut at that moment of ideal immaturity before the buds swell. Thus I slipped into the friendly company of those who garden for good eating.

I commend this approach to all who have a little land and

a liking for poking about in the earth. We who start gardening only because we relish food at its best escape the drudgery experienced by gardeners ambitious to provide as much sustenance for the family as the plot will support. Our crops are dictated only by appetite. We are not slaves to the bumper crop, to the thrifty "winter keepers." We can experiment with this and that vegetable on a small scale, disregarding our failures and capitalizing upon our successes. We are the true amateurs of the kitchen garden. With this attitude we find that the pleasures of gardening grow upon us and are the greater because they are intimately linked with the pleasures of the supper table.

2

ARMCHAIR
GARDENING

It is well to face it at the outset: a vegetable garden is a highly personal matter, especially a garden designed to supply table delicacies for immediate good eating. The gourmet gardener is on his own, free to rule his vegetable kingdom according to his own taste. Each man's garden will be unique. Two gardeners, plying their rakes and trowels on identical plots side by side, will not have identical gardens. Even if both are planted to the same crops, one will have more beans or fewer tomatoes. One will have peas climbing on brush, the other may have them sprawling. There will be variations in spacing of rows and placing of plants. In one, the whole row of beets may be allowed to grow to plump and bulging maturity; in the other, the row may show gaps where beets have been pulled when young. Each garden will have its own character, subtly reflecting the personality of its creator.

This makes gardening exciting and rewarding, that we are free to imprint our own special stamp upon our back-yard domain. Digging with someone else in his garden may be pleasantly companionable, but it is not the same. It is poor sport compared to nurturing our own, and very tiring. Not that we ourselves scorn assistance or miss an opportunity to glean what will be useful to us. We welcome others to share in our planning and help with the spading; we freely consult books for advice and direction; we are glad to exchange ideas and seedlings with fellow enthusiasts. But we remain in charge, and with jealous pride. This is not to be deplored. This possessiveness is becoming; it is the mark of the true garden lover.

It is well to face, too, that our gardens tell a lot about us. Straight, flourishing rows, weed-free and neatly labeled, bespeak a gardener devoted, meticulous, well organized, possibly somewhat settled in his ways. Tools leaning helter-skelter against the fence, caked with dried earth? A disorderly gardener, indeed, but eying his well-cultivated rows, we may guess him to be one with little time sense, impatient of routine, or perhaps an enthusiast who worked too long and too hard and

could only throw down the tools in exhaustion. Scanning the crops in a garden, their variety and the quantities of each, we can pretty well estimate the gardener's taste in eating—though in one with a fine stand of kale and no cabbages, one may fairly suspect that the gardener is more interested in what is easy to grow than in what is good to eat.

This, then, is the outlook when we undertake a vegetable

garden. We embark upon an adventure new and stirring, in which we will be putting our signature in green-growing plants on a patch of ground, for us to enjoy and for all to read.

We may start with the vision of what is to come, but every garden must begin with a plan. Free-associating one's way through a few favorite menus and jotting down the garden produce required for the perfection of each dish is to be encouraged at this stage. It focuses the appetite on herbs handy for selective seasoning, on crisp greens to inspire the most creative tossing of a salad, or on the convenience of being able at any moment to pull a carrot, leek, or onion for soup or a ragoût.

Consider a menu appropriate to the peak of springtime: chilled vichyssoise made with leeks, a crown roast of lamb filled with bread stuffing delicately seasoned with onion, garlic, celery, rosemary, thyme, and parsley, and to garnish the platter, watercress and basil jelly. The accompanying vegetables: buttered young onions and new potatoes. And, since it's spring we're dreaming of, asparagus hollandaise. No salad, but a bowl of raw vegetables would not be amiss: strips of carrot and green pepper, celery, scallions, radishes, and cauliflower. Something light and refreshing is required for dessert, perhaps strawberries chilled in curaçao and scented with a sprig of lemon mint. Twenty garden items on this menu alone.

Some of the twenty are of course quickly discarded when the second step of garden planning is undertaken: the practical consideration of space, time, and energy. Watercress rightly needs a brook, though tub culture can be successful. Potatoes need space; celery and cauliflower are tricky to raise. Asparagus?

Space again, and three years before the root system has gained strength enough to tolerate generous cutting. Strawberries? By all means, but one must reckon the time and attention they require.

Responsible books on vegetable growing emphasize the importance of studying space, time, and energy—usually in that order. Their approach makes sound sense when the goal is maximum production, with surplus to can or freeze. My own theory of gardening for the sake of table specialties for immediate consumption calls for studying these factors in reverse order. For first of all, this kind of gardening should be fun, and what you enjoy doing is just what you have most energy for.

Time runs energy a close second in importance. Salad greens and a few undemanding root crops like onions, carrots, and beets had best content the weekend gardener. If, however, an hour or so a day can be dedicated to the vegetable patch, plus a good Saturday workday, one is ideally situated to garden. Weeding and cultivating are not arduous taken little by little, pests can be spotted before they take over, and there is still time daily to appreciate the growth of comfortably tended crops.

An honest estimate of energy, considered with a schedule of available time, determines the amount of land to dig up. The garden can be large or small; my preference, and it would remain the same even if I had unlimited space, is for smallness. Sitting in the armchair before dinner, it is easy to stake out in the mind's eye a fine plot fifty by one hundred fifty feet. That plot is unequivocally too large. Better to start modestly, as one masters the scrambling of eggs before embarking upon a soufflé.

My own start was modest enough: a few herbs tucked in the flower border, a row of lettuce edging the garden path. From this it was a short step to converting part of the cutting garden to a salad garden. That summer, in an area roughly four by eight feet, we crowded six tomato vines, staked and tied to conserve space, and two rows of lettuce, with clumps of herbs

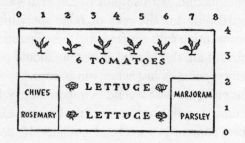

at each end of the rows. We even boasted an early crop of radishes and scallions planted in circles around the tomato stations.

The success of this venture drew me on. Each year has seen the cutting garden dwindle and the food garden expand, until at last it has reached the limit of available space. Now raspberries grow along the fence formerly festooned with zinnias. Two grapevines climb the garage wall; clumps of rhubarb flank the rose trellis. Beside the birdbath at the far end of the lot, mint grows in a sunken tub. The vegetable patch itself is still small; it could be stretched only to about fifteen by twenty-five feet, since I was unwilling to uproot the rose trellis and to sacrifice the perennial borders. But it is sufficient for my small household. Salad makings are still predominant: tomatoes, cucumbers, peppers, herbs, lettuce, and the scallions and radishes that can be interplanted anywhere. We have broccoli for Gino's sake, and leeks for stews and vichyssoise. There is room for a few each of the old reliables—onions, carrots, and beets. We have peas during their short season, and snap beans from July to October. Each year I change my garden a little, for the sake of trying something new. Given more land and a little more time, I would add corn, asparagus, strawberries—and butternut squash.

But the variety and usefulness of this small garden surprises me afresh every year. We never lack salads, from the May days of radishes, scallions, and lettuce thinnings to the first hard frost, when still-ripening tomatoes are brought indoors and green ones fried with sausage for Sunday breakfast. We have feasts of raspberries, tomatoes, broccoli, beans—and of beets and carrots, which I never thought to be feasts until I savored the difference between market-bought and home-grown.

Once the size and general character of the garden are settled, the real fun of gardening begins—still in the armchair—with graph paper, pencil, and a stack of catalogues, drawing up the garden plan.

And of catalogues I do mean a stack; one will not serve the purpose. As a beginning gardener I found it useful to check back and forth, guessing that a variety listed in all my catalogues would likely be a reliable grower and safe to try. With experience I learned to watch for name varieties. Seedsmen vie in developing their own special strains, and I like to order from the originator, who has a stake in maintaining the quality of the seed that bears his name. One often has to hunt for what one wants—the new All-America selections, for example, or rosemary or chervil, which are not always listed in every catalogue. Browsing through the catalogues, I read with fascination the capsule descriptions of new strains developed at one or another agricultural experiment station, catching a vision of the vast programs of research and experimentation quietly carried on by our governmental services to improve the quality of the seed we gardeners use.

This process of selection, consulting the lists of "musts" and "wants" and "let's trys," and comparing them with the offerings of the catalogues, is one of delicious indecision. It involves many rough drafts as I succumb to the seductiveness of catalogue pictures and descriptions and then am caught back to the tight reality of my pint-sized plot. I may feel a pang of regret, but the smallness of my garden is a protection. Without its strict limitations, the catalogues would undoubtedly charm me into undertaking more than I could manage.

__ check with garden center and watch garden magazines for names of seedsmen and nurseries . . .

__ easy does it . . . five postcards—investment of fifteen cents and ten minutes—equals five handsome catalogues . . .

__ an order for even a quarter's worth of seed keeps me on the mailing list . . .

__ graph paper ruled in squares of five lines each makes easy garden planning . . . 1 square = 1 foot . . .

3

JIGSAW-PUZZLE
PLANNING

Figuring the best location for various crops is one of the most entertaining jigsaw puzzles of armchair gardening for a small back yard. Space must be conserved to the utmost if we are to have variety and a steady supply of sweet young vegetables. Sun and shade and the lie of the land are basic determinants. The eventual height and spread of our crop selections must be considered, so that tall growers will not be so placed as to shade the ground huggers. Patterns of growth and length of time to maturity—in these matters the catalogues are reliable guides—are important in figuring interplantings and succession sowings. Cucumbers, for example, I place between plants they can climb on or spread into—tomatoes on one side, perhaps, and on the other the patch of peas, which will be harvested before the cucumber vines begin to sprawl in earnest.

Even the convenience of the gardener is a consideration. I find it practical to group tall-growing, all-season vegetables at either end of my garden, since they can be left to their own devices much of the time. The middle section I devote to "repeat" crops which need more attention, such as snap beans, carrots, beets. Lettuce and herbs, of course, must be placed for handy picking.

Sitting snug by the fire while the snow lies, one can ruminate for hours on these matters without putting pencil to paper. Such ruminations pay off; they save many false starts and lead us confidently to the practical business of getting the working plan on paper. Mine usually shapes up with a simplified version of the graph shown on page 31. My garden runs lengthwise from east to west, so I start my plan with the tall growers, tomatoes to the east, broccoli to the west. My fifteen-foot rows can accommodate ten tomato plants and a dozen broccoli. For broccoli, Italian Green Sprouting is the standard variety. This is a most satisfactory vegetable to grow, for after the first heads are cut, small ones sprout from the lateral branches, and we cut and cut until freezing weather. We cook these tender tips on a bed of lettuce in a covered skillet, with butter and no extra water added. The result justifies growing your own broccoli.

The tomato row, however, poses the question of choice. We like them best sliced raw with basil, or halved and baked with herbs. Rutgers fills the bill for shapely globes of scarlet, solid-fleshed and full of sweetness, fruiting bountifully right up to killing frost. Marglobe shares top honors with Rutgers and ripens a trifle earlier. Jubilee, once an experiment, is now a stand-by; its heavy yellow fruit, mild and non-acid, gives pleasant contrast to a platter of red tomato slices topped with rings of onion and green pepper. A couple of Red Cherry tomato plants supply us with a munching bowl most of the summer, and what is better at the cocktail hour?

Thus appetite dictates our selections: we have three plants each of Marglobe and Rutgers, two each of Jubilee and Red Cherry. Next to the tomatoes, but a good four feet away, go the cucumbers, with a space for a garlic corner at one end. Four cucumber hills, each with four or five seedlings, will, if the season is favorable, yield a crop almost too bounteous for a family of two, except for those of us who never tire of cucumbers—in sour-cream dressing, in mayonnaise for cold salmon, sautéed like zucchini, or just plain with salt. I have had excellent luck with Burpee Hybrid and with the 1957 All-America selection, Smoothie.

Dill comes next on the garden plan, and then three rows dedicated to the all-season repeaters: onions, beets, and carrots. Dill has become as much of a summer necessity to us as basil; besides its usefulness with cucumbers and tomatoes, there is the ritual of potatoes roasted in aluminum foil, pinched open to receive sour cream and a sprinkling of fresh-cut dill. To stretch the season for all of these staples, I plan for plantings of five feet each at about three-week intervals, beginning in mid-April. The dill flourishes into September; the root vegetables we dig young and then reseed for a late crop.

I find myself dwelling upon the virtues of onions, carrots, and beets, which most people consider lowly vegetables. Never are they to be found in market in the size or condition that does them justice, for they are at their best when too small for profitable marketing and, like corn, lose their sweet and delicate native flavor with keeping. Undersized onions mild for creaming; carrots small enough to cook tender in butter in less than ten minutes; baby beets to boil and chill and dip in curried mayonnaise—our back yard garden furnishes these delicacies luxuriously.

Since we grow onions to eat and not to store, I buy a pound of the more perishable white onion sets and keep planting them until they sprout in the bag. I put them in the onion row almost touching one another and, when they shoot up, start eating them as scallions to thin the row, letting every fourth onion mature. Another whole row of onions—for scallions, and to cook like asparagus—can go at the far edge of the garden, beyond the broccoli.

For beet seeds, I find it a toss-up among Crosby's Egyptian, Detroit Dark Red, and Burpee Redheart. I'm always experimenting with carrots: Oxheart is ungainly; Goldpak grows straight and shapely in our well-pulverized soil; Tendersweet and Nantes Half-long are sweet-flavored and have indistinct cores.

Beside the carrots are the herbs. Here, particularly, the dic-

E

N 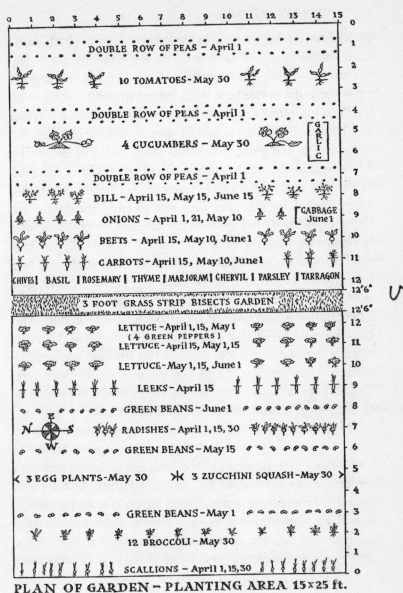 S

0 1 2 3 4 5 6 7 8 9 10 11 12 13 14 15

DOUBLE ROW OF PEAS – April 1

10 TOMATOES – May 30

DOUBLE ROW OF PEAS – April 1

4 CUCUMBERS – May 30

GARLIC

DOUBLE ROW OF PEAS – April 1

DILL – April 15, May 15, June 15

ONIONS – April 1, 21, May 10   [CABBAGE June 1

BEETS – April 15, May 10, June 1

CARROTS – April 15, May 10, June 1

CHIVES | BASIL | ROSEMARY | THYME | MARJORAM | CHERVIL | PARSLEY | TARRAGON

12'6"

3 FOOT GRASS STRIP BISECTS GARDEN

12'6"

LETTUCE – April 1, 15, May 1
(4 GREEN PEPPERS)
LETTUCE – April 15, May 1, 15

LETTUCE – May 1, 15, June 1

LEEKS – April 15

GREEN BEANS – June 1

RADISHES – April 1, 15, 30

GREEN BEANS – May 15

< 3 EGG PLANTS – May 30   >< 3 ZUCCHINI SQUASH – May 30 >

GREEN BEANS – May 1

12 BROCCOLI – May 30

SCALLIONS – April 1, 15, 30

PLAN OF GARDEN – PLANTING AREA 15 x 25 ft.

W

tates of taste must govern what and how much to plant. Armchair dreaming about food leads us on—sometimes too far, as my own herb row has taught me. When I first started to grow herbs seriously, my zest for them led me to plant eight feet of basil and five each of my favorites, rosemary, marjoram, thyme, and chervil. I had half a row of parsley, with the remainder sowed to dill, and a clump of chives at the end. The only thing I was right about was the chives. I had far too little dill, and of the rest an overabundance, more than I could use or give away. Since I have neither time nor patience for drying my herbs, I quickly started to revise the schedule for the herb row. My current plan gives me a separate full row of dill; one row suffices for all the rest. I have whittled down the footage to two feet each for thyme, marjoram, rosemary, parsley, chervil, and basil. These I treat as annuals and sow every year; they give ample thinnings and snippets for us and for our neighbors. The basil thrives so lustily that I have learned to plant it at the north end of the row and to allow only the two sturdiest seedlings to mature. These reach a height and girth of nearly three feet. The herb row is rounded out by the clump of chives and a root of tarragon given me by a fellow herb enthusiast.

This herb row is at the mid-point of my vegetable patch; a three-foot strip of grass bisects the garden, leading from the rose trellis to the birdbath at the back fence. Across this path are three rows devoted to five kinds of lettuce. Salad Bowl, even if it were not such a superb leaf lettuce, I would grow just to look at, so charming is its frilly rosette, which spreads opulently almost two feet across. Matchless, another leaf lettuce with much of the buttery quality of Bibb, is as indispensable as Salad Bowl; both last well in the heat of summer. Bibb, compact of growth and a good autumn grower, is another staple of my lettuce rows, and I have small patches of Oakleaf, with its bronze-tinged leaf, and of Great Lakes, which tries its best to head. I use Great Lakes, a glossy, brittle lettuce, for Caesar Salad instead of romaine, which has too often failed me.

Next to the lettuce is a row of leeks. Leeks (London Flag) are so easy to grow and so hard to find at market when you want them that I always wonder why so few home gardeners raise them. Young leeks make a pleasant change from scallions and are provocative when cooked like asparagus and dressed with hollandaise. They add subtlety to soups and stews. This leek row and the lettuce rows are cheated a foot or so at the north end; there, staggered between the rows, I put four green pepper plants, of the variety California Wonder. Their presence doesn't affect the early lettuces; it is only by mid-August that the peppers grow bushy and towering.

Beyond the leeks is one row for snap beans, and then the space I keep for trying new things. One year it was okra, which produced too few pods at a time to be worth the space it took; another year I flew in the face of reason and tried artichokes. I produced nothing edible, but the vegetable flowered spectacularly, the choke a spiky cushion of periwinkle blue. I have tried kale and chard but discarded them quickly, since neither of them do I really enjoy eating. Recently I have experimented with eggplant and zucchini, both of the same name, Black Beauty. I can count on two or three mature eggplants—and they are black beauties—from a bush with thirty blossoms; three plants are enough to satisfy our taste for eggplant. The zucchini

33

Black Beauty is another 1957 All-America, a prolific bush squash. Three plants of this gave us a magnificent harvest. The handsome dark green fruits thrust out from the stem from late July until frost blackens the plants. These zucchini are most delicious when cut young, no more than five inches long, and preferably three or four; but if one escapes my notice and grows to fourteen inches or more, it is still buttery and tender.

And so we meet the broccoli at the west end of the garden.

This is the basic garden, but the tally is not yet complete. There are the peas and more snap beans to consider, quick-maturing vegetables ideally adapted to companion planting. Peas we always try, although unless they are in early—St. Patrick's Day is traditional in our area—and the growing season just right, they may fail. By allowing a little more space than is actually needed for the slow-growing tomatoes and cucumbers, I can work in three double rows of peas (Wando is my first choice, otherwise Greater Progress or the old stand-by, Little Marvel) for a small feast of this queen of the early vegetables. Snap beans, except for the one row beside the leeks, are a movable crop in the garden. Early plantings are made on each side of the eggplant and squash; by the time these are reaching for sun and lebensraum, the beans are finished and the plants ready to pull out. By mid-June some of the early lettuce and onions will have been used up, and I can begin planting short rows of beans wherever a bare space emerges. This practice may give the garden an air of dishevelment repugnant to the meticulous gardener but endearing to those of us who prize beans above beauty.

Wade had always been my first choice for snap beans, but

after a trial of the 1957 All-America, Greencrop, I shifted my allegiance. We like snap beans in their infancy, slim as straws, cooked whole and served with a dribble of butter and lemon juice. Both Wade and Greencrop are superb in this stage of immaturity. If, however, a rainy spell keeps us out of the bean patch and the beans overreach maturity before we can pick them, Greencrop has a decided edge over Wade. Wade tends to toughen and become fibrous when the seeds grow big; I have picked the flat Greencrop beans ten inches long and found them still tender and tempting to the palate.

And radishes. I tuck them in anywhere, in circles around the areas reserved for tomatoes, broccoli, eggplant, squash; between the rows of slow-germinating carrots and beets; as markers among the herbs. The chief charm of the radish is that it pops up so fast—four weeks from planting to eating. It is the gardener's first cheerful token of a new season's bounty. This disarming attribute has taught me to like radishes; I've tried White Icicle, Cherry Belle, and the new Champion, which I find no better than Cherry Belle except in size.

It may take several armchair sessions to scale up the working plan, make decisions about which, how much, and where, and finally to write out the modest order for seed packets and plants and record these for reference in the seasonal garden log. But they are hours well invested by prudent gardeners, who know they must be prepared to take quick advantage of whatever gardening weather spring may decide to bestow. The time will soon come to spade up the garden the first day the soil is crumbly enough to work. Then will begin the schedule of planting and the rhythmic cycle of thinning, cultivating, weeding, fer-

35

tilizing, watering, and spraying—a cycle to test our devotion as gourmet gardeners. But at this stage of armchair gardening that's still well in the future. At the moment we have it on paper, in all perfection, for the garden of the mind's eye knows no weed or pest or disease; it flourishes in soil effortlessly rich and loamy, under skies never darkened by clouds because it rains only on Mondays and Thursdays from 1 to 6 A.M.

❨ JOTTINGS FROM THE GARDEN LOG

__ cucumber seeds keep, can be used a second year . . .

SEED ORDER

__ Beans
| *Greencrop snap beans* | ½ lb. | 1 packet sows 20 ft. 3 packets should do. Safer and only 5¢ more to get half pound |

__ Beets
| *Burpee Redheart* | 1 pkt. | sows 20 ft. |

__ Carrots
| *Tendersweet* | 1 pkt. | sows 30 ft. |
| *Nantes Half-long* | 1 pkt. | |

__ Cucumbers
| *Burpee Hybrid* | 1 pkt. | 30 seeds |

___ Herbs
  Parsley   1 pkt.   sows about 40 ft.
  Basil   1 pkt.
  Chervil   1 pkt.
  Dill   1 pkt.
  Marjoram   1 pkt.
  Rosemary   1 pkt.
  Thyme   1 pkt.

___ Leeks
  London Flag   1 pkt.   sows 25 ft.

___ Lettuce
  Bibb   1 pkt.   sows 40 ft.
  Great Lakes   1 pkt.
  Matchless   1 pkt.
  Oakleaf   1 pkt.
  Salad Bowl   1 pkt.

___ Onion sets
  White   1 lb.   sows about 60 ft.

___ Peas
  Wando   1 lb.   ample. 1 lb. sows
                               100 ft.

___ Radishes
  Cherry Belle   1 pkt.   sows 25–30 ft.
  White Icicle   1 pkt.

__ Squash
Zucchini Black Beauty   1 pkt.   sows 8–10 hills

__ add to seed order 1 pkt. each Cabbage, Golden Acre, and Chinese Cabbage Michihli. Try for late crops.

PLANT ORDER

__ Broccoli
Italian Green Sprouting 12 plants

__ Eggplant
Black Beauty   3 plants

__ Peppers
California Wonder   4 plants

__ Tomatoes
Marglobe   3 plants
Rutgers   3 plants
Jubilee (yellow)   2 plants
Red Cherry   2 plants

__ Chives   1 pot from grocer's

4

A WHIFF
OF
SPRING

That first deceptive sniff of spring, borne in on the breath of a February thaw, brings a delightful shiver of anticipation of spring in the garden. There's no time to lose, I find myself thinking, if I'm to be ready for spring planting. I'm wrong, of course, about spring in February, but I'm not wrong about the value of advance planning for the garden.

Zones of frost east of the Rockies. Based on the average dates of the last killing frost in spring. There is a variation of several days within the zones themselves. From U. S. Dept. of Agriculture maps Base map © Rand McNally & Co. Chicago—R.L.5533

The working plan, by now neatly ruled off with exact measurements of distances between the rows, is only the first essential. Next step is to make a rough estimate of planting dates, including a plan of succession sowing—in my garden, frequent

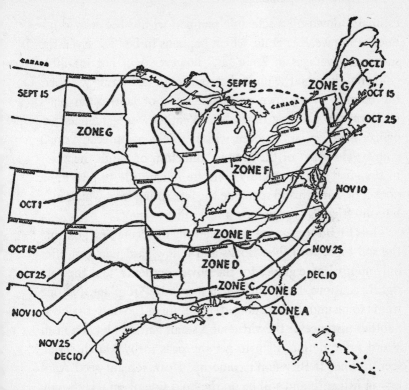

Zones of frost east of the Rockies. Based on the average date of the first killing frost in the autumn. The dates may vary from year to year. From U. S. Dept. of Agriculture maps
Base map © Rand McNally & Co. Chicago—R.L.5533

sowings in five-foot stretches is one answer—to prolong the season of harvest. Days to germination, to maturity, must be verified, and the qualities of "hardy," "half-hardy," and "tender." I spared myself much trouble when I learned to set my

estimates down on a schedule planned within the frost dead-
lines of my weather zone, which happens to be "F." Even the
statistical averages of Zone "F," however, will not infallibly
guide me through the unpredictabilities of our spring weather:
the climate of my own particular nook of land often plays
tricks on the planting timetable. Weather-wise gardeners rec-
ognize great variations even within this geographically small
county; elevation of the ground, direction of winds, nearness
to the great lake frequently conspire felicitously to give me a
pocket of warmth and spare me the late spring frost which may
bite my friend's garden only a few miles away.

Thus I tend to plan for early planting of vegetables, granting
the soil to be workable. Books and fellow gardeners can offer
only approximate guides for the novice gardener, and they are
rightly cautious in advising when it is "safe" to plant. No one
wants to be unduly discouraged by failure at the outset. This is
another instance of the virtue of a small garden plot: one can
afford to be daring. Plan to get the peas in by March seven-
teenth, fine. If they don't come up, I can replant seed April
first or fifteenth and still be on the bold side of safe, with only
an hour's effort and a few seeds wasted. In any case, young
plants are sturdy and mostly take the nip of a spring frost in
stride. If on some still, windless night with the temperature
dropping fast a really dangerous late frost is heading in, I can
ward off damage by sprinkling the garden at night. This is to
me a mystifying recommendation, but I am told that sprinkling modifies the interaction between cold and warm air and
helps the plant tissue maintain its content of moisture. Or I

can try covering the young plants with newspaper tents weighted down with stones.

However, all my plans for early planting may be upset if the weather stays soggy into April. The condition of the soil, not the fear of frost, must always be the determinant of spring planting time. A warm, sunny day may tempt me, but if I squeeze a handful of soil and it remains a solid lump, I must wait to spade up the garden. Only the lily of the valley, which finds its way to bloom through the blacktop of my driveway, could pierce the cement-like clods of a garden worked up when the soil is still wet. A late, wet spring may tantalize me, but I can comfort myself that a delayed start doesn't really matter too much. As weather warms, the seedlings can be trusted to catch up with nature's timetable.

A satisfying way to study the seasons is to keep a five-year garden diary in which to jot down weather, planting times, seed varieties selected, dates of harvest, and suggestions for another year. This is no dull task. Sometimes there are daily entries for as long as two weeks at a time when the season is young or crops are at their peak. Usually, however, keeping the garden

log requires but a weekly notation, a review made in leisured comfort on the terrace. From year to year the comparisons are instructive—and appetizing. Pleasant family rituals can develop if one jots down in the diary menus concocted to set off one or another garden specialty. The ripening of the first cucumbers, for example, is in our household a signal for a supper featuring cold poached salmon *en gelée*, cucumbers in sour cream, and blueberry pie.

The checking of tools and supplies is another valuable bit of advance planning for the busy spring gardening season. Peat moss, sand, superphosphate, ground limestone, and a commercial fertilizer of 5–10–5 (five parts nitrogen, ten parts phosphorus, five parts potash) or 4–12–4 analysis can be stocked while the snow lies. By March I am hunting manure, and if I'm lucky I can buy a couple of bushels at a dollar apiece, to

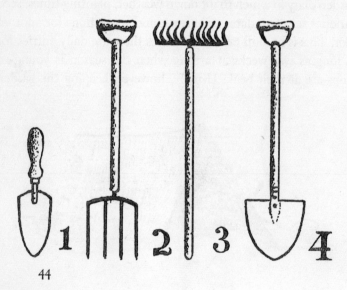

hoard in the garage against the first good gardening day. Others may sniff and sneer, but the dedicated gardener well knows the virtue of well-rotted manure and welcomes its fragrance as a fore-runner of spring.

Tools are another matter. They must be kept clean and bright, and their care is a tiresome chore at day's end. Lazy gardeners like me do well to keep tools at a minimum. The first season I made out very well with only five: spade, spading fork, rake, trowel, and a deep-bellied garden cart. Most people would wish to add a hoe and a long-handled cultivator, but I like to get down to earth and do my weeding and cultivating with the trowel. I prefer the garden cart to a wheelbarrow—though I now have both—because it can be maneuvered with one hand and is easily tipped to spill its contents on compost pile or garden row.

5

Certain planting accessories are needed and can be laid in early: a ball of stout string for lining up the rows, and twelve-inch wooden labels which serve as stakes to anchor the lines and as a record of the varieties sown and the dates of planting. The household yardstick can be borrowed for measuring the distances between rows, but I find it convenient also to have stakes cut to twelve-inch and fifteen-inch lengths for quick spacing of the narrower rows. Six-foot stakes for the tomatoes, and chicken-wire supports (brush is almost impossible to find in our well-manicured suburb) for the pea vines are early essentials; they should be put in place before ever a pea is put in the ground or a tomato plant set out. Flats and jiffy pots or plant bands, and whatever sowing medium one prefers, such as vermiculite or perlite, will be wanted when the fever of the season is upon us. One may add other necessities—spray guns, dusters, watering can, hose and sprinkler, Twistems, and as many shapes and sizes of baskets as one can collect. But these are for later and need not darken the springtime horizon.

Gadgetitis is an ailment common to gardeners and gourmets. The companionship that exists between these two high arts, solidly grounded as it is in enjoyment of good food, is manifested in many directions. The passion for top-quality produce, the respect for the tools of the craft, the sense of adventure which leads us to try things new and exciting—these common traits mark the companionable arts. And they have weaknesses in common as well. Otherwise sensible, prudent men and women may enter garden-supply shops to buy a packet of seed as innocently as they enter delicatessens to buy a loaf of bread. Then gadgetitis sets in, and they come out with arms full and pockets empty. No one questions the allure of garden shops and delicatessens, and the sin of succumbing to their charms is forgivable. But it can go too far. Why buy a dibble for planting when a pencil makes a perfect hole? I discipline myself by applying to garden purchases a principle I laid down years ago in the kitchen. I ask myself three questions: Will this utensil do the job better? Will it have many uses and be used frequently? Is it worth the shelf room and the care it requires? I have in the garage a "sadder and wiser" shelf whose crowded disorder testifies that my self-discipline has not always been all it should be. Each year, hopefully but usually vainly, I promise myself that this shelf shall be cleared before the day of the first spring break in weather.

❲ JOTTINGS FROM THE GARDEN LOG

TOOLS AND ACCESSORIES. . .
KEEP TO A MINIMUM. . .

__ essential tools: spade, spading fork, iron-tined rake, trowel . . .

__ also useful: hoe, long-handled cultivator . . .

__ garden cart or wheelbarrow? . . . cart gets my vote, but nice to have both . . .

__ supports for pea vines . . . brush hopeless to find in this manicured suburb . . . simple support: chicken wire (18-

inch) stapled to 3-foot stakes . . . can be rolled up and stored when not in use . . . use at least 4 stakes to each row or wire will belly and sag . . . allow extra footage of wire to turn in around end stakes so skirts won't snag . . .

__ tomatoes . . . 10 six-foot stakes . . . Twistems, 12-inch . . .

__ labels . . . 12-inch painted wooden labels best . . . tall enough to escape mud spatter . . . under $3.00 in lots of 100 . . . one lot lasts several seasons . . . 6-inch pot labels also useful for seedlings . . . tongue depressors handy in a pinch . . .

__ jiffy pots a real find for starting cucumbers, squash, etc. . . . no setback in transplanting . . . pots disintegrate as roots push through . . . about $2.00 in lots of 100, round or square . . . get smallest size; one lot a 3-year supply for me . . .

__ couple of flats to hold jiffy pots . . .

__ string and 2 round stakes for guideline . . . use sections of old broom handle, make one end pointed . . .

SUPPLIES FOR STARTING GARDEN
FIRST YEAR . . .

__ manure . . . let's splurge with 4 bushels . . . in general, barnyard manure can be spread 3–4 inches deep but I never can afford that much . . .

__ peat moss, 1 bale . . . or compost, 6 bushels . . . can be spread 2–3 inches deep . . . almost impossible to put too much humus in vegetable garden . . .

__ ground limestone (agricultural slag) . . . 15 pounds . . .

__ superphosphate . . . 15 pounds . . .

__ fertilizer . . . 4–12–4, 25-pound bag . . . 20 pounds at start, balance for side dressings later . . .

__ sand . . . 100-pound bag . . .

5

GOOD
GARDEN LOAM

That day in spring when I can scoop up a fistful of earth and feel it crumble and spill between my fingers as I open my hand marks the beginning of a new season of garden plenty. The soil in my garden is black and friable, giving promise of the delicacies it will yield for summer eating. Tomatoes, plump and ruddy; green beans dressed with dill; freshly pulled carrots to munch raw; pungent herbs for the shish kebab marinade—standing on the bare earth, I can already savor the flavor, texture, and fragrance of what will grow where I now stand.

Now, after six years of building up the soil of this garden, spring preparation is relatively simple. A week or so before we can expect to start digging we spread compost and peat moss on the earth left rough from the fall turning. When the day comes, we fork it all under, digging each year a little deeper to add inches to the workable soil, and give it a maintenance dose, say ten pounds, of fertilizer.

The achievement of "good garden loam" is one of the solid satisfactions of gardening; one may take as much legitimate pride in it as one does in the creation of a superlative ragoût. My garden began as solid-packed clay, full of rocks, rubble, and stubborn-rooted weeds. That first spring there was no possibility of scooping up a handful of soil; leaning my full weight on the spading fork in an attempt to loosen the unyielding earth, I despaired of growing so much as a radish.

I had been well advised to consult experts, and Paul W. Dempsey (*Grow Your Own Vegetables*) and the Blairs (*The Food Garden*) sustained me through the first heroic efforts to ready the garden for planting. The plot was too small for anything but hand spading, which meant that the first upheaval was a backbreaking job. We took the digging in three stages. After the first spading we tossed on the garden a dressing of fifteen pounds each of ground limestone and superphosphate, two bushels of manure, and about a bale of peat moss, and then left the plot rough for a week. By the second week the big clods had dried out enough to break up small, and we

52

worked in twenty pounds of 4–12–4 fertilizer and a hundred-pound bag of sand. The third week the part of the garden which was to be planted first was ready for the final preparation of raking and pulverizing. In those early days, if the chemical krilium had been on the market and my purse heavy with gold, my work would have been lightened. I could have worked this soil conditioner, in powder form, into the topsoil of the vegetable patch to make the caked earth crumbly, as I have since done for shrubs and bare patches in the lawn.

Drainage demanded my attention. My kitchen garden is at the wet end of the lot, and that first spring one corner held water so long that it got me off to a slow start. Luckily we did not have to lay tile; a dry well corrected the difficulty. We excavated a hole three feet across and four feet deep and filled in two feet with rocks and rubble dug out of the garden. This we covered with enriched earth and topsoil. In this moist corner the raspberries and broccoli and squash do very well. As for the rest, repeated working in of peat moss, sand, compost, and manure has over the years raised the surface of the garden soil several inches above ground level, so that in spring the earth dries quickly to workability.

One may take rightful pride in a garden raked and glistening, ready for planting. Every spring I like to stop for a bit and survey my small domain, bare now, but soon to be barred with green sprouts and ultimately so clothed in green that no earth will be visible. Now, I realize, my advance planning has paid off, saving me time and trouble in the long run, and enabling me to take the spring rush in easier stages. The working plan, the schedule of planting dates show me at a glance, on any good gardening day, which packets to pull out of the grape basket I use for a seed file, which section of the garden is to be planted, and how much footage for this particular sowing. The tools and materials are at hand; I can load the garden cart with rake and trowel, string and stakes, and get down to the job with dispatch.

Peas are the first to go in, preferably by April first at the latest. In this climate I have long since given up trying for a prolonged pea season by planting early and medium varieties in addition to Wando; a cold late spring followed by a sudden onset of hot weather has too often ruined two thirds of my crop. Radishes and lettuce go in soon after the peas. For the other hardy "regulars"—onion sets, carrots, and beets—I aim at April fifteenth or earlier for the first sowing and mark on the calendar the dates for successive sowings at three-week or one-month intervals. Leeks, parsley, dill can also stand sowing as early as April fifteenth. Snap beans are usually safe to plant in my garden early in May, the rest of the herbs by May fifteenth.

Since I don't have a cold frame or a window sunny enough

for starting tender vegetables, I buy tomatoes, peppers, broccoli, and eggplant as seedling plants and celebrate Memorial Day by setting them out. Cucumbers and squash I do grow from seeds, starting them in early May. Because these vegetables do not transplant happily, I use plant bands or jiffy pots (one can even use paper cups with a hole poked through the bottom) to start them in—one seed to a pot, which can later be transferred to the garden without disturbing the roots of the young plants. I range these starting pots in flats and set them on the garden path, where they may drink in the spring sun and rain while the ground is still too cold for their comfort, and whence they can easily be removed to the garage at night if frost threatens. Memorial Day is their day, too, for permanent placement.

The planting of seed has tricks beyond the directions on seed packets, as I have gleaned over the years from practice and from the exchange of gossip with gardening friends. I like to be meticulous about planting seed in straight rows and at the proper spacing. Because my soil is clay-based and holds moisture well, I tend to plant seed less deep than the seed packets recommend. Tiny seeds like carrot I barely cover, sometimes giving them a sprinkling of sand before patting them firm. Larger seeds, such as the beans, go in one inch deep instead of two.

Plant thinly, the packets say, and this I do to some extent to save the necessity for drastic thinning later. But I find it safer, in a small garden, to be generous with seed, so that I can allow the sturdiest seedlings to remain and have some allowance for transplants if a section of the row comes up scanty.

55

+ this is great

Two or three seeds to the inch are recommended for lettuce, carrots, radishes, and dill; I plant three or four. The seeds of the other herbs are so tiny it is almost impossible to space them and, being brown, they are immediately invisible when dribbled from the hand. By mixing the seed with dry sand, I can get a reasonably even distribution.

I am not fussy about furrows and drills when I plant my seeds. Once the guideline has been stretched, I make a shallow groove with the rake handle (lay it on the line and step on it), tear off a corner of the seed packet, and tap gently to spill the seed as evenly as may be. Run a finger along the groove, drawing in loose soil from the edges, and the seed is at once distributed and absorbed into the topsoil, so that a quick tap with the back of the rake easily gives it the firming that it needs.

We take such delight in the early salads of lettuce thinnings that in recent years I have worked out a variation in lettuce planting which gives us a bigger yield of these delicate little shoots. I make the groove for the lettuce rows three inches wide and broadcast the seed crosswise and lengthwise; come thinning time, I pull seedlings from the outside and manage to leave a fairly straight row at the center of the lettuces that are to mature.

A planting device I have recently found successful is to water the newly seeded rows with liquid krilium. A cupful in my three-gallon watering can, sprinkled in a narrow band along the guidelines, takes care of two rows, encouraging germination by settling the earth evenly and holding its moisture. Since I have tried this I have had far less trouble with crusting and cracking of the surface soil when a dry spell follows a hard rain.

56

try this

Lettuce + Cucumbers
early

With beets I am at pains to spread the seeds apart, so that there are only about two to the inch. Since the wizened, oddly shaped seeds—which are really fruits—will send up several shoots, each one of which will grow to beethood, crowded sowing is not for beets.

The leeks get special attention to provide for proper blanching of their fat stalks. For them I prepare a V-shaped trench about six inches deep and scatter the seeds in the bottom. A little earth, dribbled on, is enough to cover them, and I settle them in by pressing along the center of the V with the edge of my hand. Spring rains will gradually fill in around the sprouts, until finally, with thinning and cultivating, the row will be level with the rest of the garden.

Peas, beans, and onions get special treatment too. I plant the peas in double rows four inches apart. For none of these three do I bother to make a groove with the rake handle. I find it easier to lay them along the guideline (peas and onion bulblets about an inch apart; the beans, two inches) and poke them an inch into the earth with my fingertip, tamping them down with the flat of my hand as I go along. With my early plantings of peas and beans, some of the seeds may fail to germinate if the season is unduly cold and wet. I watch for the sprouts as they first break through—one year I waited six weeks and was about to give up, when suddenly the whole row sprouted. If, after the first seeds sprout, two-inch gaps show in the pea rows, or four-inch ones among the beans, I fill them in promptly. This extra effort I don't grudge, for in my small plot, if I am to feast on these garden-fresh delicacies, I cannot be content with a skimpy stand of crops.

Nor can I waste any space between rows. To get maximum production of what I like to eat, I crowd the vegetables as closely as I dare. Double rows of peas, the charts say, should be six inches apart; mine do very well on four-inch spacing. I shade the minimum recommended distance—twelve inches—between rows of carrots, beets, and lettuce. Radishes, since we pull them young, I can cheat to eight inches. Snap beans still bear prolifically when the rows are but fifteen inches apart instead of the proper minimum of eighteen inches—in fact, at fifteen inches the plants seem to prop each other up.

Broccoli, zucchini, eggplant, peppers, tomatoes, and cucumbers, although early in the season crowded by interplantings of peas and beans, mature with their full share of space, which ideally should be thirty-six to forty-eight inches. However, I place the tomato seedlings only eighteen inches apart instead of twenty-four, and the broccoli fifteen instead of eighteen, in order to accommodate as many plants in a single row as possible. All of these vegetables, when I transplant them on Memorial Day, are set more deeply in the soil than they grew in their flats: I trowel out a hole deep enough to allow their first leaves to be almost at ground level and water them well to encourage the growth of side roots from the seedling stems. For this watering after transplanting I use a starter solution of two tablespoonfuls of complete fertilizer to a gallon of water.

I have often wondered by what tortuous bypaths of semantics the word "hill" has become the accepted term for the depression in which one plants cucumbers. As a novice gardener, I was trapped by the literal meaning of the word. I built up two little mounds of earth, put four seeds to each hill as directed, and waited for the cucumbers to come up. Beginner's luck in the form of a wet season was with me; come up they did, in profusion, climbing all over the tomatoes and bearing a bumper crop. It took a drought the next season to set me straight: "hills" should be wells to catch rain and to make for easy watering of the thirsty vines. Cucumbers are greedy about food as well as drink; they relish a rich diet of fertilizer, preferably manure, and they like it best in liquid form. I have found that the most economical way to cater to their likes in a small garden patch is to give them a real well. At transplanting time I sink a flowerpot in the soil and pack it with manure,

either well-rotted fresh manure or one of the dried varieties like Driconure. It is then a simple matter to feed and water the cucumbers at the same time by pouring water from the watering can into the flowerpot, thus liquefying the manure and letting it seep to the roots of the vines.

Planting the seeds, setting out the plants, pridefully regarding the neatly aligned rows—these activities give rise to the natural desire to beat the season. To be able to serve *piselli all' italiano* before the neighbors' peas are plump in the pod; to serve up the earliest mess of snap beans with a whiff of chervil and dill from the herb row: such innocent ambitions may be natural enough, but they can lead to gestures that may prove extravagant in time, effort, and money.

A hotbed, for example, is a cherished necessity to gardeners who pride themselves on pre-season lettuce; even my inordinate fondness for a good tossed salad, however, does not tempt me to such elaborate gardening. Nor does a cold frame tempt me more than mildly. For my small garden and limited space, the convenience of handling early seedlings would not compensate for the nuisance of seeing to their proper ventilation. Even Hotkaps—those little paper plant protectors shaped like dunce caps—are not for me; they too must be checked frequently and slit for ventilation, and in my vegetable patch seem only to provide a protected place for slugs to do their ugly work. Polyethylene film, I am assured by the garden catalogues, is the answer for back-yard gardeners: ". . . clear polyethylene film over wire hoops permits earlier planting, protects from frost and wind. Ventilation openings are built in, easy to use . . ." Why spend the money, asks a knowledgeable friend, when you can get the film by the yard and make your own tent, laying the film over wire coat hangers shaped into hoops and stuck in the ground upside down by their handles? Three or four of these hoops, straddling the seedlings at right angles to the row, will support a good length of polyethylene film. This is a simple way to approximate the miniature "in-the-row plastic greenhouse" pictured in the catalogues.

COAT-HANGER-
FRAME for POLYETHYLENE
FILM

I like an early start, but I am not that eager to rush the season. Better for my casual way of gardening, I find, to study the seasons year by year, in order to give nature its best chance to do my work for me.

I make no apology for being a casual, even lazy gardener. I like to work outdoors, and I am constantly spurred on by the happy prospect of feasting upon the results of my labors. But I am no slave to scientific methods. I have never bothered to have a soil test,* though that is considered the wise thing to do. To begin with, I assumed that the soil was essentially fertile because it supported a lusty growth of weeds, and I was content to follow the directions in garden books for fertilizing a beginning garden. As for acidity, the beets signal when lime is

*For the purposes of this book I submitted soil to my garden center for analysis. They rated it A-1 on texture and composition and gave it a rating of just under $pH7$ level of acidity, which is just about what vegetables like.

needed. Every three or four years I may notice that their top growth is puny, with too much red in the leaves; that is my signal to give the whole garden a quick application of hydrated lime, which starts acting in the soil as soon as it is worked in and watered.

I don't go in for special growing media for seedlings, such as vermiculite or sphagnum moss; I prefer to use my good garden loam, lightened with peat moss and sand. Nor do I sterilize the soil or treat against damping off. I'd rather fill a few extra jiffy pots with soil and seed and trust luck.

I do have a compost pile—in fact, two, one ripening and one building up—because I can't bear to lose a bit of the humus my heavy soil needs. But it is not scientifically constructed in layers of waste material, loam, and manure, nor is it turned over as often as the books recommend. Our method is to toss on any greenery that is not diseased (seeing to it that a good layer of coarse material is on the bottom, for aeration), sprinkle it with Adco and a little earth if we can spare it, and leave it to its own devices. To be sure, it takes two years instead of one to decompose enough to crumble easily, but that's no matter when one keeps two piles going.

It can readily be seen that, in my plan, gardening is to be made as much fun and as little effort as is consistent with a top yield of pleasure at the supper table. Fortunately nature is bountiful and prolific and responds even to happy-go-lucky care with an upsurge of growth and a harvest of plenty. But nature is prolific in many ways and one must be practical. At one time I lost three beautiful cabbage heads in the space of half an hour at sundown. I had admired them late in the afternoon and had planned the menus they would adorn in the weeks to follow. One head, surely, would be stuffed according to my old French recipe, with hidden pockets of seasoned meat; we'd have a fine mess of corned beef with another head sliced and boiled very quickly, so that it stayed green and retained an edge of crispness; there'd be coleslaw for a dinner of baked whitefish and for a picnic with Canadian bacon broiled on the terrace grill. These visions danced in my head and tickled my palate. Thirty minutes later, when I stepped out to cut chives for the vichyssoise, the cabbages were gone. Only short stubs showed where they had grown. Since then my gardens have always been fenced in, sometimes with pickets, sometimes with chicken wire. I gladly play it nature's way in the vegetable kingdom, but not in the equally prolific animal kingdom. In my garden there's not room enough for me and even one rabbit.

Rabbits, who relish tender young lettuce even more than cabbages, are not the only menace to unfenced gardens. I have been plagued by overexuberant puppies and by an old dog hunting a soft berth for his bone. Small children racing after a ball, toddlers making bouquets of the pretty flowers on the eggplants, are among the hazards. No one expects the very young to be too clear about what may and what may not be trampled or plucked; a low fence is a deterrent far more effective than the most tactfully worded admonition, much less the squeal of horror at damage done, which serves only as further incitement. And besides protection, a fence can serve a useful gardening purpose. I once had a miniature garden in Connecticut, about twelve by fourteen feet; we fenced it with chicken wire and planted our peas along all four sides, thereby not only conserving space but also saving the trouble of constructing brush for the pea vines.

But cats. Fences only challenge their feline agility. How does one persuade them that the vegetable patch is no proper place for prowling and digging?

⟨ *JOTTINGS FROM THE GARDEN LOG*

PLANTING DATES

__ beans . . . May 1–15 . . .

__ beets, carrots, dill, leeks, onion sets, parsley . . . April 15 . . .

__ cucumbers, zucchini squash . . . sow in jiffy pots May 1 . . . set out May 30 . . .

__ herbs . . . May 15 . . .

__ lettuce, radishes . . . April 1 . . .

__ peas . . . March 17–April 1, whenever ground first workable . . .

__ tomatoes, eggplant, broccoli, peppers . . . set out May 30 . . .

SEED SPACING, DEPTH . . .

__ beans . . . 2 inches apart, 1 inch deep . . .

__ beets . . . 2 to inch . . . cover ¼ inch . . .

__ carrots, radishes . . . 3–4 seeds to inch, barely cover . . .

__ herbs . . . mix fine seed with dry sand for even distribution
. . . don't bother to cover, just pat seeds in . . .

__ leeks . . . 3–4 seeds to inch in V-shaped trench 6 inches
deep . . . barely cover . . .

__ lettuce . . . 3–4 seeds to inch, broadcast in furrow 3 inches
wide . . . barely cover . . .

__ onion sets . . . almost touching, 1 inch deep . . .

__ peas . . . 1 inch apart, 1 inch deep . . .

TRANSPLANTS . . . SET DEEPER IF LONGSTEMMED . . .

__ broccoli . . . 15 inches apart . . . 24 inches between
rows . . .

__ eggplant . . . needs 2 feet square . . .

__ peppers . . . need 18 inches square . . .

__ squash . . . bush zucchini need 3 feet square . . .

__ tomatoes . . . 18 inches apart, 24 inches between rows . . .

__ krilium . . . to treat top 6 inches would need 47 pounds (1 pound treats 4 cubic feet) . . . at $1.39 per pound, too expensive . . . top two inches would need 16 pounds . . . still too expensive . . . use liquid krilium, water only seed rows after sowing . . .

6

THINNINGS
FOR
THE SALAD BOWL

It is always a shock to me, flushed with the satisfaction of spring planting and of seeing the new sprouts poke through the earth, to remember that if I don't take prompt precautions my work may overnight be undone by the cutworm. I have never seen this unpleasant maurauder at work but I have turned him up in the moist topsoil, curled up comfortably for a day's rest after a night of gluttony along the lettuce rows. His greed has its useful aspect, however, for he will more readily feed on poison mash than on lettuce, and one can lure him to destruction by seeing to it that bait is spread when first the seedlings sprout. It has been my custom to buy prepared cutworm bait, black and syrupy, and turn it out with a wooden label in driblets along the rows, not letting the poison come in contact with the seedlings. One baiting is usually enough, although cutworms can be troublesome until mid-June or thereabouts. For the seedling plants I buy to set out at the end of May, I make flat collars of roofing paper—these can be kept from year to year; the plantlets I raise in jiffy pots are protected from under-

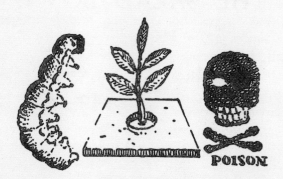

POISON

ground attack by the pots themselves. If recent reports prove accurate, however, none of us should have much trouble with cutworms in the future: chlordane, it is said, sprayed on the rows at seeding time, will forestall cutworm damage.

Aside from the cutworms, May is a month to be enjoyed in the vegetable garden. Every week is busy as the planting schedule moves along. By the time the first seedlings show green, it is time to sow seed in another five feet of the row. We must cultivate after spring rains, when the soil has dried out sufficiently; we must inspect new plants for early infestation of insects. But we work under a mild sun in the midst of spring, and can breathe deep of air filled with the fragrance of blossoms and the spicy aroma of fresh-turned earth. It is exhilarating to glance over to the flower borders, rich with the bloom of primroses and bluebells and tulips, and to look up into the feathery, many-shaded greens of the trees in new leaf. Nature has again fulfilled her promise of spring beauty, we say to ourselves, and will fulfill her promise of summer bounty from our vegetable rows, now so young and immature.

We do not have so long to wait, at that. Before we have planted the second five feet of the radish row, the first five feet are ready for thinning—to two inches apart—and before we realize it, the first crisp Cherry Belle will be plump enough to bite into.

And we eye the growth of the lettuce with high anticipation. The first salads from my garden are made with thinnings from the lettuce rows; the young plants are fragile and must be washed with great care to avoid bruising the miniature leaves, but they make a proud bowlful. The salad is our first garden plunder, except for the radishes, and the scallions—also thinnings—we've simmered and served with hollandaise.

I thin the lettuce when the seedlings are three inches high, pulling out three or four little plants every three or four inches, to make growing space for the rest. As these fill out I thin and thin again until the lettuces stand almost a foot apart. Occasionally for a flourish I pull a whole head to present to a friend, but once the plants are well grown we cut leaves from the base and let the crowns develop. There will be a fine succession of salads as the lettuce rows fill out and the greens are joined in the bowl by radishes, scallions, and chives. By mid-June an occasional young beet leaf adds color. The herbs begin to have flavor when the sprigs are two or three inches high, and I can use a few at a time to vary the character of the salad. Later there will be the cucumbers, peppers and tomatoes, and young zucchini to slice thin and add to the concoction. There need be no end to the imaginative composition of salads when one has a back-yard salad patch to draw upon for inspiration.

It is easy for the mind to leap ahead to the delicacies of summer, but in May and June thinning is the business of the moment. The peas and beans need no thinning; they were planted to the proper distance, and their problem is more likely to be gaps in the rows which need to be filled in. We have already thinned the onions to three inches apart by eating the intervening bulbs as scallions. Carrots, when they reach a height of four inches, are thinned to two-inch and leeks to three-inch spacing. The herbs I leave dense, merely pulling a sprig or two from time to time as I need them to add to stew or salad. Except the basil. As I thin that strip of the herb row, I mark two lusty seedlings a foot apart, and thin away from them in both directions. These two, which will be allowed to grow to maturity, I cut back, pinching out the tip of the plant— and later the side branches—to force a bushy, compact growth.

Except for the lettuce, herbs, and beets, thinnings aren't good for much but the compost pile. Beets ought to be thinned with the carrots and leeks, but those of us who relish a good mess of beet greens, with onion and chopped bacon and lemon juice, let them reach a height of six or seven inches before thinning the plants to three inches apart.

Thinning is a painstaking bit of handwork, a stern reminder of Kipling's verse, ". . . and half a proper gardener's work is done upon his knees." To reduce discomfort, I borrow the foam-rubber mat from the scrub closet, settle my sunglasses well down on my nose, and go to it with no tools but the trowel and the kitchen scissors. The scissors I use when the earth is very wet or when the seedlings are very thick. It is easier to snip off excess seedlings—especially of carrots and parsley—at ground level than to disturb and reset the tiny plants. For the most part, however, I pull the seedlings gently by hand, breaking up the crust that inevitably forms along the planted row; the plants that remain I settle a little deeper in the moist soil, pushing them down gently and pulling loose earth around them to prop them up. Then with the trowel I cultivate between the rows, a good three inches away from each line of plants. Later on it would be harmful to the far-spreading feeder roots to do more than stir the surface for aeration and moisture and scratch out the weeds; at this season I don't hesitate to loosen the top three inches of soil so that they may absorb as much moisture as possible in the next spring rain.

There is nearly always some disturbance to the delicate young root system when thinning is done, and the plants left in the row may wilt and be set back in their growth if the day is hot. Newspaper protection helps prevent wilting, but I try rather to do my thinning toward evening, so that the cool of the night may revive the tender seedlings.

That first salad of lettuce thinnings, whose crisp freshness proves that our efforts will be generously repaid, is well timed. It comes just when we need a breather. We have been weeding and cultivating for some weeks and we deserve some edible pickings for our labors. Let us not be afraid to admit that in spring and early summer we gourmet gardeners do labor for our good eating. Spring rains pack the soil when the seedlings are struggling to thrust upward; it takes patient work to loosen the crust after heavy downpours. The greedy weeds grow lush, seemingly overnight; it's only good sense to grub them out while they are young and shallow-rooted. But it *is* work, work that can't be side-stepped if a bounteous harvest is eventually to gladden the dinner hour.

No gardener can ever say, "There, that's done!" in May or June. There is never a "once and for all" during the season of good soaking rains. We can take heart that the need for thinning and cultivating and weeding will taper off in July and August—except for crab grass and the malevolent pussley, properly called purslane, which thrive on rich earth in hot weather. We can take heart, too, that the season of garden plenty just around the corner will make even the pussley sink into insignificance.

(*JOTTINGS FROM THE GARDEN LOG*

CUTWORMS . . . SPREAD BAIT WHEN SPROUTS SHOW . . . OR TRY CHLORDANE . . .

__ prepared bait doesn't go very far . . . homemade recipe: 2½ pounds bran, 2 ounces paris green, ½ cup molasses, 4 cups water . . .

THINNING . . .

__ carrots, radishes to 2 inches . . .

__ beets, leeks, onions, to 3 inches . . . take it in two steps: first thinning to 1 inch apart: second thinning to 3 inches

__ use thinnings: onions as scallions; radishes as tidbits; beets as greens; carrots as fingerlings . . .

__ lettuce . . . to 3 inches, then to 6 inches, then to 10 or 12 inches . . . use thinnings in salad . . .

__ dill . . . to 3 inches, then to 6 inches . . . use thinnings in salads . . .

__ rosemary . . . to 5 inches . . .

73

__ basil . . . thin away from 2 selected seedlings a foot apart . . . pinch out tip of plant for bushy growth . . . use thinnings in salad, on tomatoes . . .

__ parsley, other herbs . . . to 2 inches . . . leave dense, pulling sprigs as needed for seasoning . . .

__ peas, beans . . . need no thinning . . .

REMINDERS . . .

__ compost heap started . . . ?

__ garden fenced in . . . ?

__ keep eye out for first insects . . .

__ for fall crop of cabbage . . . sow a couple of feet somewhere to Golden Acre . . .

7

GOOD
GROWING WEATHER

As we thin the young plants and work the soil between the rows, we know that the time for summer care of the vegetable patch is upon us in earnest. Weeding and cultivating, spraying and watering are for me the least endearing aspects of gardening. Laying out the garden plan was sheer pleasure. Catching the days that were right for working up soil and sowing seed, welcoming sun and rain as the seedlings sprouted, timing the transplanting to get ahead of a spring shower—all this was good-natured sparring with the weather. But once the season settles into good growing weather, the game with nature becomes a serious struggle, a battle against encroaching weeds and devouring insects, with always the threat of drought and wet spells and the diseases they engender.

I like to keep my surface soil well crumbled, to slow down evaporation and thereby to conserve moisture deep in the earth. This cultivation is no longer the hard work it was in my early days of struggle with the lumpish clay. The humus and compost I have worked in over the years has given the soil an easy friability, and cultivating has become a chore rather than a major job. When the earth has been packed down by rain and then has baked and crusted in the hot sun, I can with comparatively little effort go over the whole patch, stirring the surface and pulling the weeds. Only the top half inch needs to be broken up; indeed, garden manuals warn that deeper cultivation would cut down the productivity of the plants by destroying the feeder roots. I am reminded every year of the virtue of shallow cultivation when, on pulling out the spent pea-vines, I observe how far-spreading and close to the surface much of their root system is.

Cultivate and weed, of course. But why more than once, some ask, when you can mulch? Many veteran gardeners recommend mulching to keep down weeds and preserve moisture in the soil. When the plants are well established along in June, they say, cultivate the earth after a good rain or thorough soaking, spread the mulch of hulls or straw or peat or grass clippings, and there'll be no further trouble the rest of the season.

True, perhaps, for large vegetable tracts, but my own experience with mulching has not been that happy. I tried straw; it blew around and made the whole yard unsightly. I tried peat; it baked solid in the summer heat and became as impervious to water as a well-thatched roof. Ground corncobs or sugar cane are hard to come by in this area. I've thought of trying buckwheat hulls, which a friend has found a great trouble saver. Coverage of an inch, he reports, keeps the weeds down and the stuff doesn't pack; it's easy to push aside the hulls and set seedlings in the moist earth below. But it cost him fifteen dollars last year to have five hundred pounds shipped to him, and this amount gave him only scanty covering for a thousand square feet. In the suburbs, where mulching materials are garden-shop specialties and priced accordingly, mulching seems to me not worth the money. Even for a small garden it requires a considerable financial outlay to spread straw six inches deep, or peat moss three, or buckwheat hulls even one inch—or to lay strips of plastic film. Plastic mulches are expensive and, to my mind, ugly. Well-tilled soil is beautiful to me; to cover it with plastic seems as distasteful as it does to slather fresh fruits with mayonnaise.

So I forgo the mulching and stick to hand cultivating and weeding, rejoicing that my kitchen garden is small enough to justify my decision. Even the weeding doesn't amount to as much as it used to. Whereas during the first season I dug out—and "dug" is the proper word—bushels of weeds, I doubt if now I dispose of more than a bushelful in the whole season.

Relentless weeding before seeds are borne has paid off; here, too, the lightening of my soil has helped, for the weeds are more easily dislodged. In half an hour or so of an evening I can go across a couple of rows, doing a thorough job of pulling weeds and loosening the rain-flattened earth. I habitually reach for a stray weed as I stroll around the garden paths. My own casual methods keep the beds clean enough.

I have learned that taking this chore in easy stages keeps it from being arduous. It is less burdensome to keep ahead of the weeds by working often, in short stretches, than to put in one whole backbreaking day and clean them out at once. It is, to be sure, a great satisfaction to look upon a garden when it is freshly cultivated and free of weeds, the neat rows brightly green above the new-turned earth, black and glistening with moisture. There's the temptation, however, to assume that the job is done for at least two weeks; actually the weeds will spring up again in two days, before one has a chance to recover from the siege.

Weeding and cultivating are the accepted lot of the small-time gardener in May and June; fortunately, as early rains taper off, this cycle wanes. But we are not let off for long. The cycle of spraying and watering waxes.

In the beginning I was unbelievably lucky. It was two years before the word got around that there was gourmet fare for grubs and insects in my vegetable garden. Aphids that flocked to the rose tips ignored the beans and cucumbers. Slugs that crawled out to eat my petunias left the lettuce alone. I wasn't even bothered by cutworms or by the wireworms I had been warned might appear the first year after sod was turned for the garden. I hope other new gardeners have this fortunate experience, for there is so much to learn about planning, planting, and nurturing the crops that it would be discouraging indeed to have to study the ways of the chewing and sucking insects and learn the symptoms of rust and blight at the same time.

When insect depredations began in earnest, I was thoroughly bewildered by the variety of pests and diseases and by the multiplicity of chemicals, dusts, and sprays recommended for their control. I studied the manuals and tried to make my own mixes, with the proper base of nicotine or arsenic, sulphur or

79

copper. But again I've been lucky. New control materials have appeared on the market, and one can buy more and more multi-purpose dusts and sprays to simplify the tedious job of coping with insects, larvae, and diseases. My chief objection now to the task of spraying is that it so often must be done after a hard summer shower, when the air is hot and sticky. Even this I can tolerate, for by the time spraying must be done frequently we are already enjoying the early salads and our spirits are buoyed by the near prospect of abundant harvest.

There are two schools of thought on how to apply insecticides and fungicides: one says spray; the other, dust. For regular treatment of the whole patch I cast my vote for dusting as being easier and quicker, with the sole disadvantage that one can't dust on a windy day. For this major operation I depend upon an all-purpose vegetable dust with a rotenone base, of which there are several varieties on the market. My best dust gun is one I bought from a rose grower: it has a fine long extension nozzle, tipped at the end to make it easy to dust the

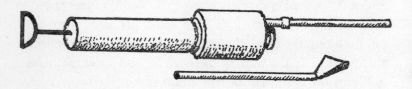

undersides of leaves without stooping; it is capacious without being heavy and it clouds smoothly with light pressure on the plunger. For spot dusting I use the flexible plastic squeeze guns, which are also all-purpose, and for spot spraying, a push-button insecticide bomb. I have learned to store my dusting powders in the house to keep them dry; the spray bomb is kept handy in the garage. I usually carry the bomb when I walk out to admire the garden, and use it casually whenever I catch a cluster of gluttonous aphids on the young tips of succulent plants, or cabbage worms making lace of the broccoli leaves.

Pest control must start early. A settled warm spell in May or early June brings the bugs out in force and stirs the so-called worms to hunger. Spray or dust twice a week from mid-May until the end of June, the books advise; keep the schedule preventive. My program is not so strict; my average is certainly not more than once a week. I try always to give the garden a thorough dusting after heavy rains to fend off blight and disease, with spot treatment for the insects as damage begins to appear. There is an impressive array of worms and maggots and aphids that pester my crops. I have not sought to learn their identity or habits; it is enough to keep an eye out for the first sign of pillage and spring for the insect gun. This hit-or-miss protection has served well enough over the years.

My real battle has been with slugs, which have now taken on the vegetable garden as well as the petunia bed. Year after year I find them lurking under leaves or in the cool shade of small clods. Nothing has seemed to discourage them, and I have often thought that the slug bait I have scattered in such quantity has served only to attract more to my yard each year from neighboring gardens. I have hope for the future, however, from the new liquid slug poison. One can water both plants and soil with it (provided, of course, that one washes thoroughly any vegetables that have come in contact with the

81

poison), thus catching the slugs either at work or at rest. It will mean an early start, for slugs are up and about in spring when the ground first warms, and I shall have to make repeated applications if the succeeding generations are to be exterminated as they appear. But it will be worth it to be rid of this repulsive and slimy garden enemy.

Pests and diseases are hard realities to test the devotion of any gardener, and one counts it a good year when they are easily kept under control. But the year that eases pest control is usually a dry year, and that poses the problem of watering. This, too, is a hot job for sticky days. It is, however, a lesser problem since the invention of the oscillator sprinkler. My new sprinkler waters the full rectangle of my garden at once with a gentle, rainlike fall. It takes about two hours—preferably on a cloudy morning—to give the garden a good soaking before I plan a general dusting.

Since I use the sprinkler sparingly, no more than three or four times in an entire summer, I haven't been much troubled by mildew and blight. Between rains or heavy sprinklings— and never oftener than once a week—I soak the ground without wetting the plants. This I know is the best way to give vegetables the abundant water they need for maturation, but it has its inconveniences. I tried a soil soaker but managed only to soak myself as well when it had to be moved. So I have gone back to the simplest method of all, which is to remove the nozzle from the hose and rest the end of the hose on a board to spread the run of water. And again luck has been with me. I have recently acquired a hose attachment which we have dubbed the octopus. It is a nozzle connection which forks

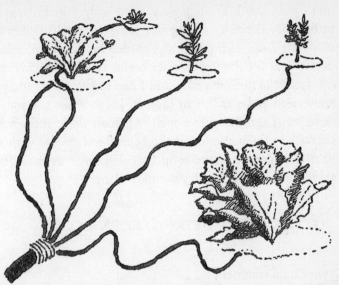

out like tentacles into five narrow-gauge plastic tubes, three of them five feet long and the two outer ones eight feet each. With this gadget, soaking the garden is five times simplified. No boards are needed, since the pressure of the water flow is divided among the five outlets. Like the open hose, it has to be moved from time to time, but this gives me a pleasant respite from work in the house.

It is one of the delights of the companionable arts that they so often complement one another in detail. During the months of summer care of the garden I frequently find myself planning my Saturdays to dovetail cooking and gardening.

The making of soup, for instance, combines felicitously with tending the crops. Minestrone or *pot-au-feu*, black bean or split pea or lentil soups are ideal for the purpose. They do not demand split-second timing; they need only intermittent attention; they flourish on long slow cooking. As I prepare the ingredients I can step out to the garden for an onion, a leek, a carrot, and for the appropriate herbs. It is pleasure to pull them from the mellow earth, and I can at the same time pull a stray weed and a radish to munch. Later, while the soup is simmering, I can do quite a spell of garden work, and when I walk back to the house to stir the kettle I am greeted with the aromatic fragrance of the soup that will await us in its hospitable tureen when the day's work is done.

(*JOTTINGS FROM THE GARDEN LOG*

__ weeds, no comment . . .

__ cultivating . . . keep it shallow . . .

__ watering . . . vegetables 90 per cent water, need abundant supply . . . thorough soaking better than sprinkling . . .

EQUIPMENT FOR DUSTING, SPRAYING . . .

__ hand-duster, plunger type, with extension nozzle . . .

__ rotenone-based all-purpose insecticide and fungicide . . .

__ squeeze-gun all-purpose vegetable dust . . .

__ push-button insecticide spray bomb . . .

8

A BASKETFUL
OF
VEGETABLES

In my childhood we used to talk with relish about "June peas."
I am beginning to think they were a myth. One year recently
we did have the first dish of peas on June twentieth, but that
was unusually early. In most years we are lucky if we can
celebrate the first peas along with the Fourth of July. "Peas,
Wando, 67 days" . . . When I first tried peas, planting them

on April first, I naïvely expected the first pickings on the dot of June sixth—on that date they were hardly in blossom. And it is not peas alone. The vegetables in my garden never seem to mature in the number of days my catalogues claim they will. My carrots and beets are seldom full grown before mid-July, although that hardly matters since we like them young—the carrots finger-size and the beets like oxheart cherries. Pulling the beets and carrots while they are still half size has an incidental advantage beyond that of good eating; it provides a painless second thinning and gives spacious room in which the remaining roots may swell to plump maturity. Cucumbers and squash come along with the tomatoes in early August.

I am now resigned to a slow timetable for all my crops and choose to blame the circumstance that my garden gets only the bare minimum of six hours' sunlight. This may be not wholly a crass rationalization of my informal gardening methods, for I have observed that the tall-growing broccoli, which the sun strikes first in the morning, and the tomatoes, which still have afternoon sunshine when the rest of the garden is in shadow, are the two plants that tend to mature on schedule.

My slow timetable, however, doesn't mean that we aren't enjoying garden produce in June. Radishes and scallions and of course the lettuce thinnings are in abundance, and toward the end of June we can pull the little white onions, thumb-size, for our first home-grown hot vegetable of the season. Since we established the rhubarb bed in the second year of this garden, we have rhubarb, sauce and pie, from early May on. The rhubarb season runs to the end of June, and it is sometimes even July before the stalks toughen and lose flavor. In most seasons we are able to combine the last of the rhubarb with the earliest saucerful of raspberries in a delectable sauce which subtly brings out the best flavor in each.

With the peas, the procession of good things from the garden begins to be a reality, and my garden basket blooms with beauty and bounty as raspberries, snap beans, beets, and sprays of herbs are added to the early greens. New shapes and colors come with the carrots and broccoli, cucumbers and zucchini, until the season is crowned by the eggplants and tomatoes and peppers, and a second basket is needed for the day's harvest.

The basket brimming with vegetables is something the gourmet gardener may revel in with justifiable pride; he is entitled to the artistic satisfaction of taking time in its arrangement. He is even to be forgiven for displaying it to the neigh-

bors on his deliberately leisured trip from garden to kitchen. I confess to a personal vanity in the matter of garden baskets, the better to show off the products of my back-yard labors. I like to collect them in unusual shapes and sizes—from the small round woven one, just right for the first half pint of raspberries, to the big square split ash basket which can house a variety of garden loot. I am also not above bringing in carrots and beets, top-growth and all, for the decorative effect of the lacy fronds and red-veined leaves, though this conceit involves me in an extra trip to the compost pile when the tops are cut off before cooking.

The snap beans, now that I have settled upon Wade and Greencrop, are the steady delight of the summer garden. We get the first of the beans before the peas are finished and, except for occasional interludes between crops, we enjoy them right into October. My beans have been relatively untroubled by bean beetles and respond to casual care, so long as I keep out of the bean patch when the leaves are wet, as a precaution against spreading rust. As soon as the beans in one row begin to taper off, we have a feast of the baby beans, pull out the plants, and reseed. In a former garden where space was not a problem I was able to let the beans have their head and thus had a longer harvest from each row, with often even a small second crop from the same plants.

Cucumbers, I find, can be disappointing. My early experience with them was one of bountiful yield, so that I began to plant only two hills instead of four. Then I began to have difficulties. Unaccountably a vine would wilt overnight, leaving visible stunted little cucumbers good only for pickling and not enough to be worth putting up. Or my vines would produce sparsely, although covered with blossoms. In the long run, however, I have garnered enough cucumbers almost every year to make me persist in trying to raise them, and I have gone back to planting four hills, as insurance; my neighbors are welcome to benefit from the superabundance of a good cucumber season.

Apparently other gardeners have had this sort of experience with cucumbers; Paul Dempsey, in his *Grow Your Own Vegetables*, comments on the increasing difficulty of cucumber culture and on the vines' tendency to go to pieces suddenly. Conscientious dusting and protection from insects with a covering of cheesecloth battened down with soil will help, he says; the former I adhere to, the latter I have tried with good success. However, my average of success with cucumbers has led me to take the lazy way and trust to luck instead of cheesecloth.

My cucumbers mystified me in another way. When the vines began to blossom they were covered with flowers, little yellow blooms nestling under every leaf. They seemed to promise almost unlimited cucumbers, yet many flowers faded and dropped off without fruiting. I ran on the explanation by chance, browsing through a garden magazine. Now when I admire the profusely flowering vines I speculate wisely on the size of crop to expect, knowing that cucumbers are like the cucurbits in bearing both male and female flowers on the same vine. This valuable bit of information is, I suppose, too familiar to experienced gardeners to seem worth mentioning; to me as a novice it was so reassuring that I pass it along to spare other novices the worry of wondering what's wrong with the cucumbers. Once I learned it, I was able to be quite calm about the zucchini squash, which generically are true *Cucurbita,* or gourds, and which perform exactly like the cucumbers. I have since learned to spot the little bulbous swelling at the neck of the female flower that betokens a zucchini soon to be ready for skillet or saucepan or salad.

The squashes have their vagaries, I found by consulting my garden center. Male and female blossoms are by no means half and half on every bush or vine. Ergo, predominantly male flowers, low productivity; predominantly female flowers, abundant harvest if pollination is successful. The best safeguard, it would seem, is to plant at least two squash bushes, thus assuring maximum pollination for the fruiting buds.

Another useful oddment of information my browsing has picked up for me is that temperature affects the setting of fruit in tomatoes. Let an unduly cold or hot spell strike when the tomatoes are in flower, and the tomato crop, as I found one year to my sorrow, will be scanty. Many flowers fall off without setting fruit when the night temperature is below fifty-nine or above sixty-eight degrees. My friends who don't want to take a chance on this misadventure spray their tomato blossoms with one or another of the fruit-setting preparations to be found at market nowadays; they claim not only bumper crops but also meatier tomatoes and earlier harvest. I am prepared to take this precaution in future if the weather forecasts make it desirable, but only in that case. The fruit-setting dust must reach the heart of the flower in order to be effective, and the effort of such precise spraying is not to my taste except in emergency. By and large, my tomatoes have yielded prolifically, and I am content.

Looking after the tomatoes agreeably offsets the dull business of garden chores that are still with us as the season advances toward the height of harvest. Tomatoes are such a dependable, handsome crop. As the vines reach for the sun one can tend them without stooping. My tomatoes grow so tall that I have contrived a trellis for them by stringing wire across the tops of the stakes and securing the stalks to their stakes and the wire with the invaluable Twistem. Tomatoes are vigorous growers, thrusting out side branches like the tentacles of an octopus. If left to themselves they could quickly overrun a small garden and one's crop might be long on foliage and short on fruit. I restrain my vines by pinching out axillary shoots as they appear. These sprout so fast, both on the main stalk and on the branches, that it takes a watchful eye to catch them while they are still small enough to nip out easily between the thumb and forefinger.

I walk along the tomato row two or three times a week to perform this rite and to watch for the tomato's king-sized enemy, the ferocious-looking tomato hornworm, which looks like nothing so much as a miniature dragon. When I meet him eye to eye as he lies camouflaged along a leaf, ready to strip it to the veins, I exterminate him with the exalted joy of St. George, uplifted by the thought that his presence means that the queen

of my crops is well on the way to fruition. There is an interesting bit of lore about the tomato hornworm: the friendly, insect-eating wasp likes to lay its eggs on him, so that the larvae may be nourished on his juicy flesh. I have only once had the good fortune to observe a hornworm bearing these parasites; the ugly monster was covered with tiny white cocoons which looked like grains of rice standing on end, like spikes. Never kill a hornworm so caparisoned. He is marked for early death, and his destroyer is a benefactor of the garden.

([JOTTINGS FROM THE GARDEN LOG

__ constant refrain in manuals, even catalogues: keep out of bean patch when leaves are wet . . . lest you spread the deadly rust . . .

__ fatten up the rhubarb patch for next year's harvest: ½ cup of complete fertilizer to each plant . . . scratch in 18 to 24 inches out from the crowns . . .

__ harvest first broccoli heads when in tight bud, close-packed as cauliflower . . .

__ fasten tomatoes to stakes every 10 or 12 inches with Twistems . . . pinch out axillary shoots . . . check night temperature; use fruit-setting hormone if below 59 or above 68 when plants are in blossom . . .

__ tomato hornworm . . . spare him when he is covered with white cocoons . . .

9

TO GO

OR NOT TO GO?

WHEN

IS THE QUESTION

Vacationing poses a delicate problem for the really ardent gourmet gardener. Of course there is no problem if one can take one's extended vacation in winter, but comparatively few jobholders can afford such luxury and I am not one of them. Especially for one who, like me, takes entire charge of his vegetable patch, vacation time is worth thought.

I have tried it all ways. By far the best from the point of view of the garden and my enjoyment of its delicacies at peak of perfection is to take my vacation in short stretches like the planting, a week here, a week there. If I keep well up on the routine work no harm ensues if I take a week or ten days off. My neighbors are glad enough to deal with a sudden influx of pests in exchange for the pickings of beans, lettuce, raspberries, tomatoes, or whatever crop is at its height during my absence.

But a whole month's breathing of other air? It is not so much a question of who will see to the planting and maintenance. That would surely be too much to ask of even my most devoted neighbor, but I can hire help and be content with what gets accomplished. The real question is: Which month will cause me the least sacrifice of good eating? September? The cabbage will be coming along all right for October feasting; there will still be all the reliable staples, plump now in full maturity; weeds are little menace and maintenance is at a minimum. But alas, the grapes and the abundance of the tomato season will be for friends, not for me. August? The month of bounty? The first cucumbers, tomatoes? Besides, in my climate in August there is frequent danger of prolonged drought. Unless the watering is systematically done, not only present crops but the fall harvest will be endangered. July, then? What, and miss the peas and the raspberries and the first fine heads of broccoli? June? The busy time of early summer care?

If I resign myself to a vacation in May, I resign myself also to a simplification of my garden plan for the season. I must

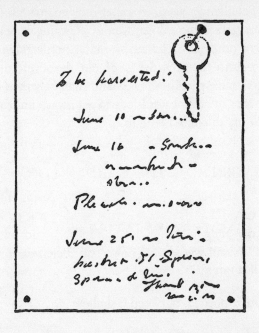

forgo much of the succession planting and concentrate on long-season and late crops. While I can make the early sowings of carrots and beets and leeks and herbs myself, I must arrange for someone to plant the cucumbers and squash at the proper time and set out the tomatoes and broccoli, the eggplant and peppers—or be late with these all-season vegetables. And at that, all may be lost if my helper thinks he can safely ignore the spraying and dusting, or weed and cultivate and thin only on the day before I return.

Perhaps it is fortunate that there is no pat solution to the question of vacation time for back-yard gardeners. It is an individual challenge. Sacrifice something we must, but at least our craft is tested, the exhilaration of planning is heightened, we discover our real preferences among home-grown specialties and plumb the true depth of our devotion to gourmet gardening. I have tried it all ways and shall continue to do so. For me it is cake both ways; I love to get away, and the garden is always a joy to come home to.

(*JOTTINGS FROM THE GARDEN LOG*

CHECK LIST, PRE-VACATION . . .

__ REMOVE all weeds . . . don't risk their rerooting themselves if it rains . . .

__ cultivate if needed, but keep it shallow . . .

__ thorough soaking, thorough dusting . . .

__ mulch, if you are so persuaded . . .

__ make list for neighbor of what will likely need to be harvested . . . give key to garage for access to sprays and dusts . . .

CHECK-LIST, POST-VACATION

__ go over accumulated mail before checking the garden . . . or you may be too tired to get to it for a week . . .

10

SUMMER JIGSAW

It was two or three years after I started gardening in earnest in this present vegetable patch that I really began to get the hang of succession planting. At first I was content to plant whole rows at a time, considering only the qualities of hardy, half-hardy, and tender in timing my sowings. I had started with a modest selection of crops suited to my inexperience:

97

carrots, beets, snap beans (in those days "string" beans, and literally so), radishes, scallions, herbs, lettuce, tomatoes, plus a flyer on broccoli. It was miraculous to see the seedlings come up and thrive and to realize that nature, given half a chance, could make a gardener of me. We did, to be sure, have to eat a lot of salad because all the lettuce matured within the span of a week or two, but we had begun to savor the heady pleasures of fresh-from-the-garden vegetables and greens.

I was dismayed, therefore, to find the garden petering out as summer progressed. Tomatoes, broccoli, and herbs were all I had left by mid-August. The bare patches in the soil I had so energetically worked up reproached me, and I was put to it to prevent the weeds from taking over.

The next summer I progressed a step, learning to stretch the season by part-row plantings over a period of weeks. But still the August gaps appeared and, deploring such waste of good garden space, I began to study succession planting. The principles I found readily in my reference manuals. Figure forward from the last frost dates in spring; add the number of days to maturity, and you will see how long your early plantings will survive. Figure what can follow what, they advised; you can't indefinitely repeat the early cool-weather crops, because they can't stand the baking heat of summer. Some of them—like spinach—you can resow when the nights grow cool, for a fall harvest. But consider the alternatives, they continue: hot-weather crops, or vegetables that will mature for fall harvesting. New Zealand spinach—if you can give it enough space—will thrive on the heat that ruins early spinach; rutabagas, which should be seeded about July fifteenth, will spurt into growth for fall digging. To make the most of your late plantings, figure back from first fall frost dates, subtract the days to maturity, and you'll come up with the latest date on which you can safely plant and expect to harvest. And select for late planting vegetables that thrive on chilly weather. So ran the suggestions in the manuals.

To adapt these principles to my own climate and the likes and dislikes of our household took experimentation. I have never bothered with spinach and I was not attracted to the suggestion about New Zealand spinach. The name of rutabaga carries no titillation to my palate. But I did study more carefully the vegetables and greens I already knew and liked.

Lettuce, for example, of which we are so fond. Many reference guides indicate that lettuce can be planted from early spring right up to July first in Zone F. Two or three tries taught me that in my particular corner of Zone F I might just as well quit spring planting of lettuce in early June: beyond then the young plants, cool-weather fans that they are, dislike finding themselves subjected to our hot, dry July air when they sprout. The June-first-planted lettuce will, if the season is favorable, carry me almost to August, and there is then only a short gap until we begin to get the thinnings of the lettuce planted for fall consumption. I can risk such sowings any time after August first when the nights cool and lengthen, but I do best, I find, if I wait until August fifteenth. We never try for a large harvest of fall lettuce; a few feet here and there, the equivalent of about one row, is sufficient, because in September and October we are concentrating on the fat, mellow tomatoes. But the fall lettuce does well. I have found tight little heads of Bibb nestling safely among wind-blown leaves even after a hard frost.

There are short gaps, too, in the season of beets and carrots. From June first to July fifteenth I don't plant beets, for they have never developed well for me in hot weather. Half a row or so planted in mid-July gives us a modest supply for bortsch for autumn days. Carrots—they too feel the heat in this climate—get their fall planting July fifteenth and will grow big enough for our tastes even when planted as late as August fifteenth.

Snap beans are the mainstay of succession planting. Monthly plantings from mid-May to mid-August can assure the gourmet gardener a steady supply—enough to test his ingenuity in concocting recipes to vary the good eating of this garden stand-by. Luckily for my family—for one can tire even of snap beans—my small garden plot could not sustain such a steady flow without sacrifice of other delicacies we relish. A glance at the harvest profile on page 113 will show that we do have beans from early July to frost, but because of short-row planting we get

5

them in waves. The first three sowings are bunched within six weeks because the beans are interplanted with the broccoli, eggplant, and squash; we must take our main bean harvest early so that the full development of these other vegetables will not be stunted. This gives us our first wave of beans in mid-July, when the first and second plantings overlap for a week or so. Another wave of overlapping maturity comes in August; from then on the beans are something we watch for every few days. Sometimes there are enough for a fine solo dish of buttered beans when friends come to dine. Sometimes we get enough for a casserole, the beans stretched out with celery and mushrooms, with a rich topping of crumbled french-fried onions. If there are only a few, they go into a salad of mixed cooked vegetables.

Figuring back from average dates of first frost is only part of the challenge of keeping the garden busy all the time. One must seek the good late growers, and in this quest there is adventure for the gourmet gardener: finocchio, turnips, and the cabbage family—cabbage, Chinese cabbage, broccoli, cauliflower, brussels sprouts, kale if you must. These are bonus crops for the gourmet gardener, fun to try, and no great loss if they fail. I have tried all of them, except brussels sprouts, as a change for the palate, but I now tend to stick to cabbage, with occasionally a half row of white turnips, which we like creamed with a fat capon.

Turnips and even kale can be sowed around July fifteenth for a late-October crop, and Chinese cabbage August first. I have had only fair success with Chinese Cabbage Chihli. The Chihli thinnings are not palatable for salads because of the furry texture of their leaves when young; too often the plants flop over and wilt just at the point when they begin to head up. But I haven't given up on this delicious salad green; I shall try Michihli, for which greater dependability is claimed.

The good late growers of the cabbage family must be sowed early if they are to be used as August fill-ins. In my early gardening days this caught me unawares. Now I prepare for it. In early June I look for bare spaces—perhaps in the onion row, where the earliest planting has already been greedily enjoyed— and sow them to cabbage. Even a couple of feet sowed to the small-headed, quick-maturing Golden Acre will yield a dozen sturdy seedlings to transplant, in August or when they are six inches high, wherever there is room for them. In my garden this is usually in the gaps of one of the lettuce rows, if I have remembered not to sow them to late snap beans, or perhaps in a part of the cucumber patch or among the carrots and beets. My experience with Golden Acre has been happy; there is a fine, buttery quality to the tender heads which far outrates any market cabbage.

We can also have a reminder of spring with late radishes. I usually tuck some in during August, and if the season is suitably moist the radishes pop up as plump and juicy as their June sisters. August, too, is the time to try the radish Black Spanish, queen of the winter radishes.

Planting seeds and transplanting seedlings in the hottest part of summer call for techniques different from those we use in spring. One trick I have discovered for my August sowings of radishes, lettuce, beans, carrots, and beets is to sow more deeply than I do in spring; I plant the seeds in furrows an inch—even two inches—deep. When the seeds sprout, they are less likely to be roasted in the August sunshine, and their rootlets can reach down for the moisture deep below the surface soil. Watering is of course a must for them, and it is well to give the furrow a good soaking before planting the seeds, as well as to sprinkle the row when the seed is sown and covered and patted firm. I try to give the newly seeded rows a daily sprinkling with the watering can, just along the guideline and without washing the grown plants nearby. Vegetables sowed in August are especially benefited by a first watering of liquid krilium, which seems to hold moisture in the top quarter inch of soil even under a broiling sun.

Watering is even more important for August transplants than for August seeds, for they can otherwise be severely checked in growth. I try to transplant my Golden Acre seedlings on a cloudy day, or at least at dusk, in order to give them the cooler air of night for recuperation. I give them, too, a deep reservoir of moisture by pouring water in the holes before transplanting; this is even more important than watering them after they have been transplanted. If they droop next day when the sun strikes them, I protect them with berry baskets or tents of newspaper. When we work against time—in this case the time of first frost —anything that can be done to assist growth to continue uninterrupted is worth while.

In August my garden takes on a look very different from the tidy appearance it presents in June and July. The broccoli, and the eggplants with their handsome pendent fruits, stand tall and straight; the mammoth fans of the squash leaves splay out in a three-foot circle; tomato vines are lush with foliage and fruit; the cucumbers sprawl comfortably in all directions. Except for the leeks, and the herb row which by now makes a pretty edging for the grass strip, the garden is patchy, with here a nearly full row of beans and there bits of rows with cabbages, beans, carrots, and beets in various stages of growth. Self-sown dill is apt to be waving its fronds above the cucumber vines— I like these volunteers for their sturdy stems and vigorous growth. In the middle of a short stretch newly seeded to beets there may be one late Matchless lettuce, its base securely rooted in the beet row, its tufted head resting rakishly against a bean bush a good three feet away, with its bare stem, long since stripped for salad, curling like a serpent across the intervening rows. The net effect of the garden may be blowzy, but every inch of the ground is at work.

August is a time of quiet satisfaction for the gourmet gardener. The peak of spraying and dusting is past; weeding and cultivating are tapering off. In a lucky year there are good August rains to make watering less of a chore. This is the month of plenty, repayment for all the hard work of spring and early summer. We can enjoy the fruits of our labor, even be a little smug about them. Stepping out to the garden for the day's plunder is a happy rite, one which I like to take in leisurely fashion, savoring future delicacies as well as present ones. Hunting a couple of cucumbers for the evening salad, I glance over at the gleaming eggplants, note the reddening of two especially fine tomatoes, and promise myself a Greek casserole with lamb two days hence. An examination of the beans tells me they should be our favorite size in three or four days; meanwhile we had better finish up the last of that strip of carrots to make room for some of the late lettuce. So many good things coming along; we have only to determine which is at its height of perfection for the supper table.

This is the pay-off of the philosophy of gardening on a small scale for immediate good eating. There is always something just right for the picking and seldom too much of any one thing at any one time. My friends who have ambitious gardens are caught in the fallacy of the bumper crop and find themselves eating to the point of boredom or spending hot August days freezing beans by the bushel or putting up tomatoes by the gallon. My grasshopper attitude toward the kitchen garden spares me such slavery to superabundance. I feel no envy of the stores they lay away for winter; I am content to garden for pleasures of the palate in the present.

(*JOTTINGS FROM THE GARDEN LOG*

__ broccoli . . . cut while heads are in tight bud . . . don't let it flower . . . if it does, it's worth only for compost pile . . .

__ herbs . . . trim back when they show bud and let blossom in house as nosegays . . .

TO KEEP GARDEN BUSY . . .

__ transplant Golden Acre cabbage seedlings in bare spaces, August 1 . . .

__ sow Chinese Cabbage Michihli, August 1–15 . . .

105

___ half row turnips, Early White Milan . . . ?

"LET'S TRYS" FOR ANOTHER YEAR . . .

___ finocchio . . . will fool friends in a relish dish . . . looks like celery, tastes of anise . . .

___ brussels sprouts? . . . cauliflower? . . . tricky to grow . . . would need to start seed in June for August transplants . . .

___ radish Black Spanish . . . winter radish par excellence . . .

106

I I

THE
GARDEN
LOG

Since this is an honest report of personal experience with a
back-yard garden, I must confess that I have not always been as
virtuous as I advise others to be in keeping up with the garden
log. In spring, buoyed by enthusiasm for the budding season,
I am reasonably conscientious. In the lazy days of summer I am
apt to let it slide, trusting hopefully that I couldn't possibly

forget the date of the first tomato or the number of zucchini my Black Beauty produced in a week. There are gaps in my five-year, five-lines-a-day diary which, if filled in, would give me a better perspective on the gardening seasons and a more reliable yearly guide to the idiosyncrasies of my climate and of the crops I grow. Planting dates are of course important, and they are perhaps the most scrupulously kept of my records; less full are the notes on dates of first picking, and even less full are the dates when harvest ended or the plants were spent.

I particularly wish I had kept a more methodical weather record of the six years of this garden so that I could look back and see more clearly how drought and rain, winds, hot spells, and cold spells affected the progress of my vegetables. Cryptic, infrequent notations are enough. "June 10—cold; rain all week" . . . "June 23—still rain . . . low o.k. for tomatoes" . . . "July 15—no rain for two weeks" . . . "August 15—still no rain, high eighties all week" . . . Such notes, compared with even scanty entries on the state of the garden, tell me a great deal about that season's heavy, early crop of tomatoes (I must have kept up with the watering in July), the quick growth and early bolting of the lettuce, the impoverishment of the raspberry season by the depredations of thirsty birds. Such notes I do have but they are all too spotty.

While I am solidly convinced of the value and interest of a well-annotated gardening record, I have still not found the perfect method for a casual gardener like myself, dedicated to the proposition that gardening should be pleasure, not burden. My five-year diary gives me comparative data for several years, but its five lines cannot always accommodate all that needs to be entered on a given day. To my indolent temperament a page-a-day diary is frightening. The year I tried one its many blank pages reproached me, and my records grew scantier and scantier, until by July 1 I had given up.

Part of the problem is accessibility. A garden log should be at elbow when the impulse to make jottings grows urgent. In my case this occurs when I drop down on the terrace for a few moments' rest; at such a time, reviewing the morning's work, I am minded to write it all down in the just pride of accomplishment. But my terrace is open to the sky, and to interrupt my relaxation to go into the house to fetch the log would be unthinkable. I have not become wholly resigned to being victimized by my own procrastination, however. Obviously the keeping of the running record would be solved by a weatherproof log box tucked under the terrace bench.

Last year I experimented with a vegetable garden profile, and I think this will be the answer for regular recording of essential information. I plan to shape up a large chart like the one on page 113 at the same time I lay out the garden plan and prepare the seed order. When the spring work starts, I shall tack it to the peg board in the garage, with a pencil securely attached. Since I have to go to the garage to store the tools after work, it will surely be no trouble to check off dates of planting, sprouting, and maturing, and to indicate the state of weather and temperature. I can visualize myself creating a code for this record—such as "P," planted; "S," sprouted; "F," first picking; "L," last picking; "RIP," crop failed—and only hope that I don't end by making the simplified record too complicated to follow.

However one keeps records, midsummer is a good time to check them over with an eye to next year's planning. Which variety of lettuce did we like best, and did we have enough of it? Are three rows of lettuce really more than we want? If so, what shall we substitute? Spinach, perhaps? Chard? Or shall we have an extra double row of peas? Perhaps one row of lettuce will suffice and we could try a two-foot strip of strawberries. Shall we give up all the beans and carrots and beets and onions and see what a few rows of corn would yield? If the peas have failed, was it because of the variety or the weather or pest or disease or neglect? Is it worth it to keep on with eggplant, when it is comparatively a space-waster for the crop it produces?

Every gourmet gardener must wrestle with his own soul—and palate—to decide such weighty questions, but the evaluation is part of the fun of gardening for good eating and is most provocative when we are in the midst of that good eating. Standing in the garden last August, I bethought me that we had had far too few boiling onions and far too short a season of them. Next year, I told myself, I shall try some from seed as well as from sets, to prolong the season. I was also inspired to try some from seed then and there, in a section of the lettuce row, for fall scallions. I had no luck. The seeds didn't even sprout. A pitying friend told me that onions are at best tricky to grow from seed and that they sometimes don't do well even when planted in spring. But I am not deterred. Next season will see me try Sweet Spanish from seed, and I shall get them in very early, along with the peas.

Such venturing on something new has been one of the continuing joys of my back-yard vegetable gardening. The first eggplant, plump and gleaming—what triumph! The discovery of the flavor of zucchini four inches long—what adventure for the palate! Even the humdrum old stand-bys like carrots and beets become exciting as one tries first one variety, then another, until it is possible to settle upon the one best suited to the tastes of the household.

Even the failures and errors have interest. The summer I tried okra, I thinned to four plants, far too few, as it turned out, to give us a worth-while crop. They bore, to be sure, but never enough for me to gather more than a pod or two at any one time. But the beauty of the white waxy flowers was spectacular, and so was the speed with which the flowers, once in blossom, developed into pods. Okra as a crop may have proved a failure, but at least I know it will grow in this climate and that a dozen plants would be needed to give us an occasional supper dish of stewed okra and pods enough for gumbo.

The fun of experimenting can be contagious. One day I found a wooden label mysteriously inscribed "Arsh Ptats" stuck in the earth near the back fence. I asked my helper, George, about it. "Mrs. Matson, I just thought you might like a nice mess of Irish potatoes, so I planted a few eyes." "But they need sun, George. They're right in the shade of the neighbors' lilacs." "They'll grow, you'll see." They sprouted beautifully,

and every week George went first of all to his potato patch, to weed and cultivate and hunt potato bugs. But as the shade of the lilacs thickened, the vines weakened and grew straggly, and one day George silently pulled them out and cast them upon the compost pile.

"You think maybe mint would grow there?" George arrived next week with a rooted sprig each of lemon and spearmint. This experiment was highly successful, although it cost us a lot of trouble to begin with because we weren't prepared for the exuberance with which the mint tried to take over the whole garden. After fruitless efforts to keep it in check by pulling out the spreading suckers, we finally penned it in an old galvanized iron tub, with the bottom knocked out, sunk to the lip in the soil. The mint flourished for a season or two, then grew spindly, and it wasn't until some years later that I learned the trick of inducing thick growth within such confined space. Each spring now, before growth starts, I chop deep into the matted mint roots with the spade, crisscrossing my strokes to cut up the root lengths. Each joint of root sends up a shoot, with the happy result of a fine thick bed of mint. We keep the mint cropped back (with the hedge shears) even if we don't need it for culinary purposes; if the plants are not permitted to flower, they stay thrifty all season.

⟨ JOTTINGS FROM THE GARDEN LOG

I like to keep a garden profile of my harvests . . . see next page . . .

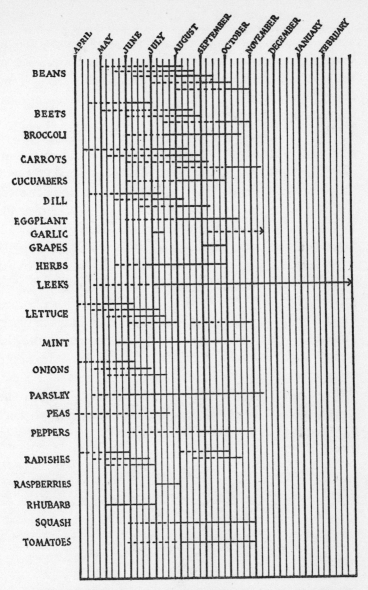

PLANTING & HARVESTING CALENDAR

----- Planting and growing time ——— Harvesting time

12

MIDSUMMER
NIGHT'S DREAM

As I mulled over the good things of the garden that day last August, a wild desire flashed into my mind: somehow I must make room for strawberries.

As the idea took hold, I started exploring it, reading, conferring with fellow gardeners, checking with the garden center. At first it seemed utterly impracticable. Not only would the limitations of my space and the sacrifice of some of my crops be involved. The standard biennial strawberries, those huge beauties we revel in every June, are more trouble than their short season warrants, I was told: you plant one year and pick berries the next; it really means keeping two beds going to have berries every year. And at that, you'll have them for only three weeks or so. Not worth it in so small a plot. Besides, there are the runners to manage and the little new plants to set. Better try ever-bearing strawberries; they'll last two seasons and you can start over again with runners. One friend urged me to try an aluminum terrace bed, which could be set on the lawn in order not to interfere with the vegetable patch. Another suggested that I try her method of using ever-bearing strawberries as a border for the rose bed. You can enjoy the scent of the roses as you sample the flavor of the berries—an irresistible combination, she assured me.

Neither of these devices appealed to me. I have no rose bed, the perennial borders are crowded as it is, and I don't want anything in the middle of my pleasant little oval of lawn. Strawberries for me would have to mean a sacrifice of some well-loved garden item—the broccoli, perhaps? Or the squash and eggplant? Surely not the tomatoes, nor the cucumbers.

Gradually my decision has crystallized and my plans are set. The broccoli will go; we have enjoyed it for six years and can afford to skip it for a season. The two-foot-wide strip thus released will accommodate thirty plants, allowing a square foot for each—thirty pints of berries, if the statistics on strawberry yield are to be believed. Even fifteen pints would be welcome. I shall buy Red Rich Ever-bearing, a patented strawberry, variant of the well-known standard, Fairfax. It is reported to be a thrifty grower and a heavy bearer and to have a "distinctive strawberry flavor." It has the further advantage that it can be ordered from a nearby nursery, so that I am assured of plants acclimated to this area.

My friends and advisers have given me tips on strawberry care, enough to fill pages in the garden notebook. . . . Any good garden loam will do for strawberries, but dig in some manure two weeks before you set the plants. . . . You'll want to give them a side dressing of 5–10–5 fertilizer in late August, about a pound and a half, scratched in. . . . Set them out early, by April fifteenth if possible, and be sure the roots are well spread out and that the crowns are set exactly level with the ground. . . . They'll start blossoming before you expect them to—almost as soon as they send out new leaves. Then you'll have to keep busy cutting off the blossoms and runners; don't neglect this, it's a twice-a-week job until the end of July, and most important, for the plants must develop strength for heavy bearing. . . . You MUST keep the strawberry bed sprinkled if it gets dry, or the growth will slow down and you won't get as many berries. . . . You aren't expecting to put up quarts of jam, I hope; in that size bed you'll be lucky to get enough for supper every now and then, especially the first season. . . . Pick them in the early morning and chill them quickly, they'll keep better. . . . Don't worry if some of the berries rot in wet weather, but get rid of them fast, or mold may develop. . . . Lay a mulch of straw when the plants are young; keeps the fruit clean. . . . Mulch the plants over the winter and you will have two crops the next season—a bumper crop of early berries, starting before the standard berries bear. Then you can dig up the plants and start over again next spring. . . .

I can see a busy season ahead with this one crop alone—and the care they require is one of the disadvantages of the beloved strawberry. And I can see that I shall have to come to mulching, in spite of my prejudices. But I look forward to strawberries and cream, and strawberries with honey and brandy, and strawberry shortcake, and hope that this new venture will prove to be a "must" for the gourmet garden.

Dreaming on the strawberry project set up a chain reaction of other dreams. Why not corn? Why not asparagus? In a wink of the mind's eye I had my whole garden reorganized: asparagus in a bed four by fifteen feet (one of my neighbors feasted his family of four on asparagus from a strip two by twenty feet), ten feet for corn (sixty stalks, ten dozen ears at a conservative estimate), double the space for strawberries and there would still be room for the herbs, the tomatoes, and a row each of lettuce and leeks. A true garden for gourmets, consisting only of the big three, asparagus, strawberries, and corn—so notably perfect only when rushed from garden to table—plus the handy makings of salad and the herbs and leeks which are almost impossible to buy fresh in market.

So to revolutionize my garden would also revolutionize my theory of gardening for a little of this and a little of that and a variety of delicacies throughout the summer season. The harsh reality of my small gardening space is not to be side-stepped. It presents a painful choice. For superlative crops of relatively short season, I would be denied the succulence of my own peas and beans, the convenience of the staple carrots, beets, and

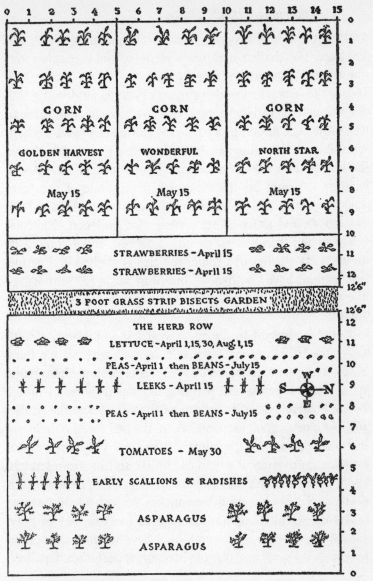

0 1 2 3 4 5 6 7 8 9 10 11 12 13 14 15

CORN   CORN   CORN

GOLDEN HARVEST   WONDERFUL   NORTH STAR

May 15   May 15   May 15

STRAWBERRIES – April 15

STRAWBERRIES – April 15

3 FOOT GRASS STRIP BISECTS GARDEN

THE HERB ROW

LETTUCE – April 1, 15, 30, Aug. 1, 15

PEAS – April 1 then BEANS – July 15

LEEKS – April 15

PEAS – April 1 then BEANS – July 15

TOMATOES – May 30

EARLY SCALLIONS & RADISHES

ASPARAGUS

ASPARAGUS

REVISED PLAN to add Corn, Asparagus, Strawberries

onions, the fun of experimenting with squash, eggplant, and cabbage. The challenge of jigsaw planning and succession sowing would no longer be mine to meet.

But the idea is not without merit. There is no denying that for the sake of variety in good eating I have forgone three of the most delicious crops a back-yard garden can yield. Perhaps flexibility and a willingness to venture on a grand scale should be one of the marks of a dedicated gourmet gardener. And a venture it would be, involving risk. If any one of the three major crops should fail, garden pickings would be slight for the season and much effort wasted. For gardeners who have space to add strawberries, an asparagus bed, and a corn patch to a variety garden like mine, the risk is negligible. For me, who cannot have "both/and" but must settle for "either/or," the idea may be tempting but the decision cannot be taken lightly.

But it is pleasant to dream. And if I should ever decide to make the shift, my garden would be well adapted for these crops. The asparagus would be the most important change; one doesn't start a permanent planting like asparagus as a whim. I could, however, easily adapt one of the far sides of the garden to asparagus—a good location, where the bed could remain undisturbed during spring spading. My soil is already mellow after six years' cultivation; it would not be like starting from scratch. But it would still be a major upheaval. Asparagus, I know, needs a prepared bed at least fifteen inches deep. I would have to find a corner for temporary storage of the top foot of good topsoil—sixty cubic feet—and would have to work the subsoil four to six inches down, digging in manure, peat moss, fertilizer, lime, and sand in the same proportions I used to start the vegetable garden. This soil would then have to be shoveled aside so that an opulent four inches of manure could be tramped down on the bottom of the bed. Then back into bed with the topsoil and enriched subsoil—in alternate layers to complete the thorough mixing—and finally a few days' rest to settle the soil and revive the gardener. Only at this point would I be ready to plant my asparagus roots.

And that means preparing two parallel trenches, spaced about two feet apart. Among home gardeners there is always ardent discussion of the proper depth for planting asparagus roots. The traditional "plant deep" is no longer considered necessary, I find. Knowledgeable gardeners have assured me that trench planting is necessary for commercial growers who use power tools but that the back-yard enthusiast can plant his roots as shallow as two inches if he will mulch the bed in winter. If you want to stick to trench planting, they tell me, five inches is right for gardens that have heavy clay subsoils; eight inches where the soil is light and well-drained. My soil is light enough now, but I do have the solid clay subsoil beneath. So I would settle on six inches deep for my roots. I would put in thirty one-year-old roots of the rustproof Mary Washington strain (it pays, I am told, to buy more roots than are needed and use only the sturdiest). These go in buds-up and roots outspread in a circle, with a covering of two inches of earth gently firmed down.

At this point I'd have to mobilize what patience I could muster. The establishment of an asparagus bed is a slow process: the first season requires curbing all impulses to sneak a few shoots to try for flavor. Soil must gradually be filled in without smothering the shoots; the bed should not be fully filled until the second season. Weeds—and how they thrive in rich earth—must be hand-pulled. Aphids and asparagus beetles must be watched for, and the stalks, which may grow to three or four feet the first year, dusted with the rotenone-based vegetable mixture. In autumn, when the feathery fronds turn yellow, the stalks must be cut off to ground level and burned.

In two years from planting, one dares taste one's own asparagus, cutting the spears just under the surface with a sharp knife. But again patience is needed; this season we are allowed to cut only for three weeks, and again the stalks must be allowed to run riot and weeds and pests dealt with. It is only in the third season that we may enjoy our asparagus to the full.

An asparagus bed is not cheap to maintain. Extravagant use of well-rotted manure, peat moss, fertilizer, and lime are needed for the start, and the asparagus is an avid feeder all its fifteen years of active production. Spring fertilizing is the same as for the rest of the vegetable patch, but an extra feeding is advisable at the end of the cutting season—one half cup of nitrate of soda for each plant—and a mulch of manure before winter sets in. However, once the bed is established, one could hardly grudge it ample nurture, for the delight it would afford. Asparagus from the back-yard garden is a proud feather in the cap. Lucky the gardener who can boast this achievement; well may he be smug, harvesting his succulent spears when other gardeners are merely planting seed.

Like artichokes in January, asparagus in May deserves a stellar role as a separate course at dinner, whether dressed with hollandaise or with butter and a squeeze of lemon. During the six short weeks of its annual harvest, asparagus lends itself to many gustatory pleasures. Alone or in combination—one I particularly relish is a luncheon dish of sliced ham on toast, concealed under spears of asparagus tips, which in turn are concealed by a coating of rich cheese sauce—asparagus is the queen of the early garden, her reign brief but gracious.

The corn patch would be less of a departure; it could be tried out for a season or two and then abandoned if it proved not worth the space and effort. The planting plan would be important because of corn's peculiarities of pollination. We are all warned against corn in single rows. Pollen falls or is blown from the tassel—the male blossom—upon the tufts of silk receptively spilling out from the ears; it then pursues the silk threads to their point of connection with the kernels on the ear, fertilizing and swelling them to their rich, milky perfection. One row of corn? The prevailing winds of summer would blow the pollen over on the bean row, where it would do no good whatever, leaving the corn kernels cheated of fruition. Two rows of corn are reasonably safe, but corn in blocks is best of all. In my garden I would want to allot at least ten by fifteen feet for corn. This I would plant in blocks of five feet each, five rows planted two feet apart. The five-foot blocks would be either simultaneous plantings of three varieties—early, mid-season, and late—or three successive plantings of the same early variety.

The catalogues—and my friends—are extravagant in praise of this or that name brand of corn, so that choosing varieties can puzzle one who wants the sweetest and most tender, with the largest possible number of ears. I have been warned not to credit all claims of productivity; two to three ears per stalk is about what to expect. I have been warned also to select wilt-resistant strains and to be sure that the seed I buy is fresh. It has also been suggested that I be prepared to read up on the habits of the corn borer and the corn-ear worm and to watch for and destroy the fat swellings of corn smut before the black fungus breaks open to spread its dangerous spores. With the dreamed-of taste on my tongue of corn fresh from the garden and the illusion of the fragrance of corn roasting, I find it easy to ignore such gloomy cautions.

Perhaps in my small garden it would be well to make three plantings—the second and third when the earlier plantings are six inches high—of Golden Midget Hybrid, which is recommended for small home gardens because it bears sweet, tender ears on stalks two and a half to three feet tall. Or should I try three varieties at once—the early Golden Beauty which is said to mature in sixty-eight days, the popular seventy-five-day Carmelcross, and the later (eighty-four days) Golden Harvest, which is claimed to be vigorous, uniform, creamier and more wilt-resistant than its parent strain, Golden Cross Bantam, which in turn is far superior to its ancestor, the beloved Golden Bantam of my childhood?

The decision would indeed be difficult; I might end by allotting another block of the garden to corn, in order to include a sampling of Wonderful, of which its purveyor says, "81 days. Here we proudly offer the tenderest, sweetest, best-tasting corn that we grow. It ripens in early mid-season, has a long harvest period, plenty of vigor, and very large yields. The long tapered ears have 12–16 rows of small, deep, golden kernels, sometimes not filled to the tips and occasionally with irregular rows, but always of WONDERFUL quality." What matter irregularity, so the quality be wonderful?

But let us be practical. Corn is a long-season crop. It must be planted when the ground has warmed up; in my climate, not before May fifteenth. In my limited space it would be wise to plant the corn two inches deep in rows two feet apart, spacing the seed kernels three or four to the foot and thinning them to stand finally eight to ten inches apart. With such close spacing, culture would pose a problem, because the young stalks should be kept weeded and cultivated and hilled up to enable the stalks to shoot out prop roots at their bases to stay them against toppling in a strong summer wind.

Corn lovers make it all sound easy. And I should like to find myself learning the sure "feel" which tells them which ears are ripe for the picking. Really experienced corn growers exhibit a touch of braggadocio by scorning to strip down a bit of husk to determine which ears to break off. They scan the browned silk tuft and run their hands up the ears gently and knowingly, seeming to feel the fat kernels beneath the husks and to sense their readiness for the kettle of boiling salted water standing ready on the stove.

Strawberries? Yes, they are decided upon. Asparagus, corn? Dreams that may yet come true.

❲ *JOTTINGS FROM THE GARDEN LOG*

TO BE OR NOT TO BE . . .

. . . STRAWBERRIES? . . . why not? . . . ever-bearing best bet for small garden—3 crops in 2 seasons, then start over . . . use plantlets from own runners . . .

    __ must have mellow soil . . . manure dug in . . .

    __ set out early . . . April 15 . . . damp, cloudy, cool weather April and May just what they want . . .

    __ keep blossoms cut off until late July . . . cut off all runners first season . . .

    __ capricious about water . . . must have plenty for vigorous growth but roots can't stand flooding . . .

. . . ASPARAGUS? . . . space-waster and short season . . . afraid not for the small garden . . . but, if added space available, a 15-year investment in good eating . . .

. . . CORN? . . . another space-waster and relatively short season . . . tantalizing to decide what to give up for the sake of having own corn . . . again, afraid added space is best answer . . . however . . .

    __ Golden Midget Hybrid? . . . Golden Beauty? . . .

North Star? . . . Carmelcross? . . . Golden Harvest?
. . . Wonderful? . . .

__ can stretch season, planting early, middle, late varieties or succession sowings same variety . . .

__ plant in blocks . . . never single rows . . .

__ count on 2 or 3 ears to the stalk . . .

__ Jake Falstaff pegged it . . . "The planting of the corn is a work which should be done with singing . . ."

I3

THE
AROMATIC
CLOVE

I learned to appreciate garlic in Italy, years before I started gardening, and promptly began to promote the virtues of the aromatic clove. "In America the name of garlic is in bad odor. Popular imagination depicts Italy as a land where every dish approaches table trailing clouds of garlic, a contagious smell which first being epidemic among foods, next infects the eaters, and finally hangs in a miasma over the whole countryside. This conception is a libel upon garlic and upon the land of garlic eaters. There are some Italian homes where, from a lack of the inmates' inclination, garlic never enters. There are innumerable Italian homes where garlic is used daily, but so odorlessly and so deliciously that no quivering nostril could take offense. Garlic is like a barking dog: most terrifying at a distance, since its smell is stronger than its taste. The unwary American sojourning in Italy at a place in which there is good cooking, and traveling thence to Austria or Switzerland or even to France, is as likely as not to miss a *je ne sais quoi*, an indefinable something, from his food. But what he misses is not a *je ne sais quoi* at all. It is the delicate and undetected flavor of garlic. . . ."*

Garlic has so far had only a whiff of mention in this record of my gardening years. It receives its brief tribute at this point because of its off-beat cycle of growth. In my first attempt to raise my own garlic, I followed the advice in the catalogues, making my planting in early spring. The flourishing green spears that sprouted led me to anticipate a wealth of fat bulbs to braid and string from the rafters to dry. My expectations were disappointed: fat bulbs I had, but in miniature, like the bulbs of the bluebell, and with no division into cloves. The flavor, however, was such as to sharpen my desire to raise proper garlic. The garlic one buys neatly packaged in cellophane is pallid in comparison with the richly aromatic, buttery, home-grown bulb. It took an Italian gardener, knowledgeable in such important matters, to put me straight. In this climate one plants garlic

*From *The Questing Cook*, by the author, published 1927 by Washburn & Thomas, Boston.

in the fall and harvests in late July, always of course saving two or three of the choicest bulbs for the next fall's planting.

This reversal of the usual spring-to-fall growth pattern is highly advantageous in my tight little garden plot. The garlic rooms happily with the cucumbers, occupying only a small corner and obligingly vacating even that when the cucumbers are minded to move in on every inch of the quarters allotted to them.

Garlic is also obligingly easy to grow. Once in the ground, weeding is all it asks for. Mine has never been bothered by disease or thrips; the slugs disdain it. Its only drawback is not its fault: most seedsmen list the bulbs in their catalogues, but it takes hunting to discover one who will offer them in less than pound lots. A pound of garlic bulbs would supply the gardens of my entire neighborhood, since each mother bulb contains eight or ten cloves. And yet, perhaps this is no real disadvantage. One can share an order with friends to start with, and once garlic is established in the garden, it provides its own sets for the next season's planting. Home-grown garlic

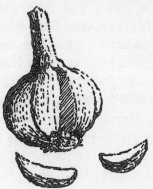

tends to make friends: over the years one usually develops a coterie of garlic enthusiasts who delight in the brisk trading of bulbs.

Mid-September is better, but October is still not too late to plant garlic. Looking over the cucumber patch for a likely spot, I remember to choose one that will not interfere with the spading of the garden in fall and spring. Either end of the cucumber row will do; a couple of feet (a dozen and a half bulbs are enough for our household) can be marked off for the garlic corner, and the garlic can rest undisturbed when the rest of the garden is worked over.

The planting is easy. I separate the bulbs into cloves and with my finger poke each one well down in the earth, three or four inches deep and about four inches apart. I cover them with loose soil and tamp it down well. To settle the soil, I give the planting a sprinkling from the watering can and then leave them to sleep the winter through. They don't sleep, however. Within a month or so, little shoots show green; by December they wave gaily in the wind, five or six inches high. At this point I tuck them up with a light covering of manure and peat moss, not so much for protection from cold, which they don't need, as for nourishment for them to draw upon.

In spring each garlic plant is a sheath of slim spears, like onion leaves; as summer draws along, I watch for them to bend and break. This, as with the onions, is the signal that the garlic is ready to harvest. Usually the bulbs are easy to pull out; if they resist a steady, gentle tug I drive the spading fork deep along the row, to loosen the earth three or four inches from the green tops to avoid injuring the bulbs. I brush off the earth, tie the bulbs in bunches by their stems, and hang them on a nail in the garage to dry. We start using the new garlic at once—the taste of new garlic is indescribably fresh and mild. When the time for planting rolls around again, I bring in the rest of the strings of garlic and hang them in a cool place in the cellar. This is a precaution lest I forget them later on, for garlic must not freeze.

It is hard for me to understand why more gourmet gardeners do not raise their own garlic. Among my gardening friends only a handful prize this flavorsome bulb as a home-grown specialty. I can only assume that many gardeners take for granted the easy store-bought garlic, not knowng what they are missing in pungency and aroma.

❰ JOTTINGS FROM THE GARDEN LOG

IF ONION SETS, WHY NOT GARLIC SETS? . . .

__ self-perpetuating . . . save 2 or 3 best bulbs for next planting . . .

__ plant September, harvest July . . . in defiance of catalogue instructions . . .

__ pick secluded corner to avoid damage in spring and fall spading . . .

__ no demands except weeding . . .

__ when leaves bend and break, time to harvest . . .

__ dry bulbs but don't let them freeze . . .

14

THE SEASON
SLIPS INTO
AUTUMN

As the season slips from summer into the crisp days of fall, gardening takes on a nostalgic tone. This is a relaxed period in comparison with the exciting days of luxuriant harvest from mid-July to mid-September, and we realize with regret that many pleasures of the palate are gone until another year. The first meltingly tender batch of peas, the incredibly sweet new onions, the first young carrots, the early lettuce that didn't bolt to bitterness until late July—these we remember with delight. The dill may have been an unaccountably sparse crop and the cucumber vines may have mysteriously shriveled and died almost overnight at the peak of their productivity, but even failures such as these provided gourmet fare while they lasted. As the shortening days limit our evening hours in the garden, we reminisce fondly about the strenuous work of spring planting and, now that cool weather dims the memory of hot sun and fatigue, even about the monotony of weeding and cultivating and spraying.

Nostalgia heightens our zest for good eating during the garden's last weeks. The peas may be a thing of the past, but the reliable snap beans are a current joy. The late fall beans please me mightily. Tomatoes, squash, cabbage—these we take for granted as the season wanes; the beans, plucked in autumn sunshine, seem to say that summer has lingered on past its time, as if reluctant to deprive us of its bountiful gifts. The last mess of beans, like the first, will deserve the distinction of being served whole, as a separate course. But this time we will dress them with hollandaise sauce instead of with butter and a dribble of lemon. The beets, swelling plumply above the surface of the soil, remind us that a salad of beets with anchovies and onion rings is a fine dish for a warm October evening, the more to be relished because we shall so soon be reduced to market beets.

We still have tomatoes in plenty; smaller, of course, than the huge round beauties of August, but sweeter than ever in the mellow fall weather. With these, the zucchini still ripening, the green peppers only recently come to their prime, and garlic and onion and olive oil, we can concoct that lusty ragoût the Provençals call *ratatouille*. The name *ratatouille* may be disparaging—it means a coarse or vulgar stew—but surely it was a name affectionately bestowed by some hearty Provençal who, in creating the dish, devised one last grand splurge with the late vegetables. For it is getting late. Will this be our last serving of broccoli tips, or will the frost hold off until a few more swell to cutting size, just enough, perhaps, to garnish a platter of lemon sole?

When October sets in, my interest in the weather reports becomes almost compulsive. We garden enthusiasts have played a game with the weather all spring and summer, but the game has a different complexion now, for the very life of the garden is at stake. The official average date for the first killing frost in our Zone "F" is October fifteenth. The lake which warms our area usually gives us a week or more beyond that deadline, and every year I try to prolong the garden season to the last possible limit. The weatherman's earliest frost warnings frequently come to nothing, but one can't afford to take a chance with the eggplant and the peppers, which are the least frost-resistant of all our vegetables. I reluctantly cut them, with some stem, when the first heavy frost is predicted. Wiped dry and stored in a cool corner of the cellar, they will keep for weeks. They are the first sacrifice. Next to go are the beans, the broccoli, the squash, and, alas, the tomatoes. Tomatoes often survive a light frost, and I can sometimes stave off the day of final harvest by sprinkling the garden in late evening when frost threatens.

For beans, broccoli, and squash, the final picking is literally

final, but tomatoes can be salvaged to provide several weeks of good eating. Any tomato that shows a yellow tinge will ripen in the house. We wrap each one separately in newspaper and spread them on a tray in a cool spot, the ones closest to ripeness in the front row for first consumption. Weekly inspection shows which tomatoes are most likely to ripen shortly, and these I range on the sunny ledge of the kitchen window to redden. This procedure is necessary for one whose cellar is warm, as mine is. My friends who have cold cellars—or heated garages —save themselves the trouble of wrapping and ranging. They merely uproot the tomato plants intact and hang them upside down. They have the pleasure of seeing first one, then another tomato turn red right on the drying vines and need only take care to pluck them off before they fall and squash on the cellar floor.

All fall we have been feasting with abandon on the sun-ripened tomatoes: sliced tomatoes, baked tomato halves with herbs, tomato-and-corn pudding, and, while the plenty lasts, spiced chilled tomato juice to drink from a tall glass with a sprig of basil tucked in at the side. Now, with frost in the offing, we can look forward to the final delight of the tomato season. Tomatoes that are hard and green I leave on the vines until the day after the first hard frost—a touch of frost seems to smooth down their puckery unripe taste—when I strip the vines in preparation for that happy ritual of autumn, fried green tomatoes. I slice them thick, discarding a thin slice at each end, dip them in salted flour, and sauté them quickly in plenty of butter. I specify butter because the slices should be browned crisp, almost to the verge of charring. Fried green tomatoes are a homely dish, and they do well at breakfast or lunch, with corn muffins and sausages or bacon and eggs. Biting through the brown crust, one encounters the unresisting soft green flesh, pleasantly tart on the tongue.

If we have not eaten up all of our cabbage heads by the time of killing frost, we treat them in a fashion similar to the tomatoes. Pull them out roots and all, is our system, and let them dry upside down on the garage floor. At the end of a week they can be wrapped in newspaper and will survive even city living until April. The secret of storing cabbage in this manner seems to be the drying out for a week; you then cut off the stems, tear off the loose outer leaves, and wrap each head tightly in several layers of newspaper. By winter's end the outside leaves may have dried to paper, but the heart, if the cabbage was unblemished to begin with, is white and succulent. It has been a long time, however, since any garden of mine has had a large enough crop of cabbage to winter over; nowadays, any heads we have left are gobbled up by Christmas.

If I have been conscientious about carrots and beets, making repeat sowings according to the planting schedule as the season went on, then we have a fine crop to enjoy in October and even into November. They must be dug up before the ground freezes. Carrots and beets can of course be stored in moist sand, but our small production doesn't warrant this, nor does the principle upon which I garden. The more mature carrots go into soups and stews; the big beets are ideal for Polish beets. This dish of grated boiled beets is easily mistaken for a dish of cranberry sauce, crimson and glistening. But one taste dispels the illusion, for the flavor of the beet is unmistakably there, tempered and smoothed by a sauce of sour cream seasoned with sugar and vinegar.

The leeks are the only crop in my garden that can be enjoyed throughout the winter. As autumn progresses, I hill them higher and higher, patting the earth around and between the fat stalks to blanch them, until by November's end only the tops of the green tufts show above the row. When the surface ground is well frozen—I want no field mice nesting among my leeks—we bank the row with leaves and prop boards against them. Thus bulwarked, the leeks are accessible all winter, even under heavy snow. We brush off the snow, push aside the boards and leaves, and break through the frosty crust of soil. The earth beneath is friable enough for us to dig free as many leeks as we may need for soup or ragoût.

Commercially grown leeks seem always to be clean to the core. Perhaps I am overly ambitious in my hilling up; my garden leeks always manage to get bits of soil wedged in the stalks at the point where the blanched, tight-furled sheaths of the stems start to fan out into green leaf. These nuggets of soil do not readily wash out. It is necessary to slit the top ends of the stalks—I usually leave an inch or two of green top-growth when I prepare leeks for cooking—with a sharp knife so that the dirt can be flushed out under a strong stream of running water.

I try always to leave a few leeks in the ground right through winter until spring. Just before the time of spring spading, I pull the last of the leeks, chop them, and sauté them lightly in

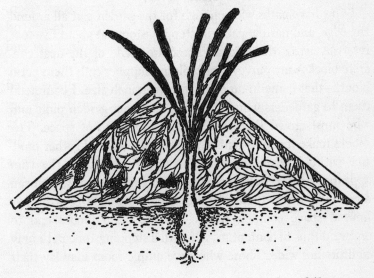

butter. I then dispose them—butter and all—in individual plastic ice-cube containers, freeze them, then pop out the cubes and store them in plastic bags. With this insurance I can gratify a yearning for vichyssoise on some hot June day when the new leek seedlings are still too young to be of value in the soup pot.

Digging leeks that first winter taught me the value of steppingstones in the garden. The first season I grew leeks, I planted them squarely across the middle of the garden. My reasoning was fair enough: I was working from the tallest crops to the shortest, so that each would have as much sunlight as possible. But it was a mistake from the harvesting viewpoint, as I discovered when I waded forth to dig up a leek or two in the mud of a January thaw. We arranged a line of rough steppingstones along the leek row, and these formed the start of a permanent feature of the vegetable patch.

I now have paths wide enough for the garden cart all around the edge, and narrow paths of steppingstones at about five-foot intervals across the garden. These are made of the neat concrete blocks—my purveyor of building supplies calls them patio blocks—that come in an eight-by-fifteen-inch size. I commend them to gardeners who have small, compact garden plots and who must crowd the rows for maximum use of space. The blocks make it convenient to plant, cultivate, and gather produce without trampling the soil, and they add to the trim appearance of a well-tended garden. Furthermore, no mean advantage, where there's a path, there's a weed-free strip. My limited space compels me to lay the patio blocks end to end, and thus to content myself with a steppingstone path only eight inches wide. Those who have ample room may lay their blocks crosswise, or splurge with paths as wide as purse and fancy dictate.

I recommend the laying of steppingstones as a November project before the final spading. With the discomfort of crouching between closely spaced rows fresh in mind, the gardener can more accurately measure off distances that make for an easy reach in both directions from the proposed path. The ground can easily be tamped flat—we used an eight-inch board and a borrowed sledge hammer—and the stones quickly laid, preferably on gravel or sand to raise them above the level of the soil and prevent heaving during the winter.

❨ JOTTINGS FROM THE GARDEN LOG

THE LIFE OF THE GARDEN IS AT STAKE . . .

__ fend off first light frosts by sprinkling the garden in late evening . . .

__ but don't take chances with the eggplants and peppers . . .

__ salvage tomatoes . . . any with a flush of yellow will, if wrapped in newspaper, ripen gradually . . . put them on a tray in a cool corner . . .

__ cabbages . . . dry them for a week on the garage floor . . . cut stems and pull off loose leaves . . . wrap in newspaper . . . will keep until April . . .

__ green fried tomatoes and scrapple for breakfast . . .

15

THE
FRAGRANT
HERBS

In general I adhere to my principle of gardening for immediate good eating by treating the herbs as annuals and giving them up to the cold when it comes. But it would be a mistake to carry this policy to extremes. In the fall, when I reluctantly turn from the gardening pleasures of summer, I'm not above trying to raise a few herbs on my kitchen window shelf. Early

October is the last call to pot herbs for the house; September is a better time. The sturdiest plants of rosemary, marjoram, and thyme may be shaped by judicious cutting back—by about one third—transferred to flowerpots packed with soil rich in humus and sand, and sunk in the ground to stay until frost. As the weather chills, I start the chore of acclimating the plants to house temperature by bringing them into the house at night and putting them out in the sun by day. The indoor time is increased as the days grow colder and shorter, until the plants are ready to stay permanently on the window sill.

I treat parsley and chives in the same way. Parsley, especially, does well in the house; I select small plants whose taproots are not too long to be accommodated in a rose pot and tuck several in a six-inch pot. I haven't had much luck with basil, which tends to get dry and spindly, and in any case makes a rank, ungainly house plant.

I haven't always been successful in keeping herbs going in pots throughout the winter. Coolness is a prime criterion for successful house culture of herbs. My sunniest window is in the warmest room of the house, the kitchen. The herbs need the sun, but they would thrive best in a temperature not over sixty degrees. A long succession of sunless days puts them at an additional disadvantage, and they develop a soft and leggy growth, lacking in stamina to push forth new leaves as I cut sprigs for kitchen use.

As for chives, they respond to the kitchen warmth with an uprush of new young spears which reach for the sun and then weakly flop over as the outer sheaths turn brown. Frequent cropping of the plant prevents the chives from thus outrunning their strength and keeps the new young growth coming, but unless I can find a cooler corner for my chives I must expect the plants to spend themselves within a month or two.

All the herbs like moisture in the air but not too much water in the pots. They do best when the pots are ranged in a tray of wet pebbles, which keeps moisture beneath them without waterlogging the roots. By this method, with weekly watering plus frequent misting from the fine spray, I can keep the plants going for a few months at least. It is well worth the effort thus to prolong the enjoyment of fresh herbs in salads, soups, and stews.

There are other autumn ways to extend the usefulness of the plants still flourishing in the herb row. This past summer I was given a nicely sprouted root of tarragon. It grew and spread, benefiting from the frequent snipping to which tarragon is inevitably subjected in our household. By mid-August it sprawled two feet across in a fine thick mat, and by September it obviously needed a crew cut to prepare it for winter. This was my signal for the making of tarragon vinegar. Tarragon vinegar and basil vinegar are to our taste the most provocative of herb vinegars and they are easily made. On a mild morning when the leaves are still moist with dew, I cut back the tarragon severely and strip a couple of plants of basil. The leaves, washed and slightly bruised, I pack about three-quarters full into pint jars. I then heat wine vinegar to boiling, using white vinegar for the tarragon and red for the basil, fill the jars not quite full, and screw on the tops. After the brew steeps for a couple of weeks, the herb vinegars are ready to strain and bottle.

Potting up an herb or two or bottling a few pints of herb

147

vinegar is about as far as I am willing to go to preserve the fruits of my garden labors. Most herb lovers dry or freeze their herbs. Of the two, if I were to depart so far from my hand-to-mouth gardening practice, I'd choose freezing, on the advice of a fellow gardening enthusiast. This adventurer in flavor has abandoned blanching herbs before freezing, as the books recommend. She merely snips dewy-fresh sprigs of various herbs, preferably at that ideal point when the buds are about to flower, when the aromatic oils are at their peak. She washes them and shakes them dry, then seals them in plastic bags—a double twist at the neck, secured with a rubber band—either singly or in combination, and in quantities just right for her favorite recipes. She warns that herbs so treated cannot serve as garnishes but that they mince easily and give the full summertime herb flavor to winter delicacies.

As for the herbs left standing in the row, if they are to winter over, they must of course be fully protected before the weather gets biting cold. One may take a chance on the true perennials—thyme, marjoram, rosemary; if they don't live, one needs only to reseed in the spring. Tarragon, since it doesn't grow from seed and can be replenished only with a root cutting, which is often hard to come by, is well worth the trouble it takes to protect it from the cold.

This job, like the general cleanup of the garden, is best done by degrees. Before the first hard frost, I trim back by one third the plants I propose to try to keep alive—and why not, indeed, freeze those excess snippets? Among the little branches I tuck dead leaves, preferably oak leaves, which will not rot and mat, stifling the plants, and I put twiggy branches around and on top of the leaves to hold them in place. As the weather grows colder, I add more leaves, and when the ground finally freezes I cover the herbs with baskets loosely filled with leaves. Weighted down with stones against winter winds, the baskets keep the herb plants snug but let in enough air so they can breathe. Thyme, marjoram, and rosemary don't get the basket, but they do get leaves and twigs.

And after the Christmas festivities we cut the branches from the Christmas tree and lay them on the herb row for a mulch. I like to think of the gay Christmas tree ending its short day of splendor in this beneficent act of protection rather than in

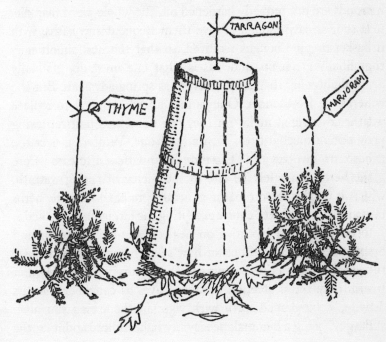

forlorn discard at the curb of the tree lawn, awaiting the rubbish collector. My Christmas trees make even another contribution to pleasant living beyond sheltering the herbs: in spring the dry branches go on the pile of kindling, and many an evening's fire is made cheery and fragrant by their crackling flame.

If my herbs fail to survive the winter, it is usually not because of the severity of the weather but because of my carelessness in uncovering the plants in spring. This is a tricky process. The herbs will begin to put forth new shoots as soon as the spring sun warms their nest—a mild spell in March is enough to start them into growth; if these delicate little bleached fronds are not properly hardened off, the whole plant may die. It sounds easy enough to give them frequent sun baths, with basket or pine boughs removed, so that the new shoots may gradually green up, and this is what one must do, gradually also lightening the leaf protection as spring advances. But the herbs are frost-tender. One cannot afford to forget to replace their covering at night, for they can be nipped past retrieving by an unexpected frost, even a light one. Wintering over the herb row involves a full two months of patient aftercare before the herbs can safely be left to the mercy of spring warmth.

It is for this reason that in general I prefer to treat the herbs as annuals, always of course excepting the tarragon. Some herbs, to be sure, seem to thrive on neglect: the chives sprout and spread every year, no matter how severe the winter may have been. One year a thrifty clump of thyme survived a cruel winter with only the protection of such leaves as caught among its twigs; it burgeoned forth with vigor in the spring sunshine. Parsley, being a biennial, needs only light mulching during the winter to grow lavish early in the following spring. For several seasons I was able to cut parsley throughout the winter by treating it to the protection of an upended bushel basket stuffed with leaves, the way I now cover the tarragon. Under that snug covering the center leaves of the rosette stayed green and crisp and were, like the leeks, cheerfully ready for plucking even on a frozen January day. However, a cold trip to the garden is hardly worth it for the readily bought parsley, whereas it decidedly is for the out-of-season leek. So I no longer bother to cover parsley for winter cutting, but rather let the sturdiest parsley clump stay in the row for early picking. When the spring-planted parsley seedlings begin to have flavor, I pull out the holdover parsley plant, for it spreads widely the second season, and when it goes to seed in July, the leaves become tough and coarse-flavored.

❨ JOTTINGS FROM THE GARDEN LOG

PROLONG THE SEASON FOR HERBS . . .

__ make basil vinegar, tarragon vinegar . . .

__ pot up for the kitchen window . . . rosemary, thyme, parsley, chives . . . small pots on a tray of pebbles kept wet . . . don't bother with basil . . . too coarse, spindly . . .

__ freeze herb snippets for summer taste in winter seasonings . . .

The Fragrant Herbs

__ winter over herb border with basket-of-leaves covering . . . or mulch with branches from Christmas tree . . .

"LET'S TRYS" FOR ANOTHER YEAR . . .

__ borage . . . for salads for those allergic to cucumber . . . likes full sun, dry, poor, light soil . . . let self-sow, plants are sturdier . . .

__ summer savory . . . salads, stuffing, scrambled eggs . . . crushed, on bee stings, will relieve pain . . . weak stems 18 inches high . . . in flower, looks as if covered with pink snow . . .

__ sage . . . too strong for my taste . . . pork stuffing only excuse . . . but pretty accent in flower border . . . gray-green, pebbly leaves . . . grows 2 feet high . . . really a sub-shrub . . . likes limy, well-drained soil . . . full sun . . .

16

DESSERTS

IN

THE GARDEN

It was in November, at the end of my first year in this vegetable garden, that I first envisioned the additions that would enhance my pleasure in the companionable arts of cooking and gardening. With the ground bare and the flower borders dormant, I dreamed of asparagus and strawberries as I do now, but soon admitted that I could not contrive the bed space they would

153

require. I could, however, perhaps make use of the boundaries of my kitchen garden. I could see the possibilities of raspberries along the fence and of grapevines climbing the garage wall. By moving a clump of chrysanthemums, I could even make room for a couple of rhubarb plants beside the rose trellis. These dreams have come true. Now, after six years, the plantings are well established and have proved the virtue of my original impulse.

I have two grapevines, one the old reliable Concord and the other also a blue slip-skin grape, Fredonia, which ripens a little earlier. For the rhubarb, I followed the usual course of gardeners and begged roots from a friend. I have the familiar pale-stemmed rhubarb, probably of the Victoria strain. For old-fashioned sauce and pie it is excellent, but if I were starting rhubarb now I'd try to hunt out one of the ruby-stemmed varieties that have handsome color and sweeter flavor.

The raspberries have been our greatest success, making every July a festival month. If for lack of space one has to choose among these three—rhubarb, grapes, and raspberries—the gourmet gardener can make no choice but the last. Raspberries are the most fragile and perishable of all fruits and, to the connoisseur, desirable only at the peak of their perfection. In one's own garden this moment can be captured. During the all-too-short raspberry season I take a daily tour of the berry patch, seeking out every berry whose translucence indicates ripeness. From the first modest saucerful to the lavish quart-at-a-time I can pick at the height of the season, I exult in the beauty and delicacy of this aristocrat among berries and mourn not at all the zinnias that made way for them. I have two varieties of raspberries, the standard Latham and Indian Summer. The latter ripens a week or so later, which stretches out the raspberry season, and of the two I consider it vastly preferable aesthetically: the berries are firm and round, whereas Latham has a tendency to crumble.

Grapes, rhubarb, and raspberries are planted in spring, but they must go in early and we were well advised to prepare the beds in the fall. This is heavy work at any time, but it is easier in autumn, when the ground is mellow and moist. Since they are all three permanent plantings and can be expected to yield generously for fifteen years and more if they get a good start, one must be spendthrift with energy and material in preparing their growing space. The beds need to be dug deep—eighteen inches at least; we dug ours two feet for good measure. We were lavish with manure, both spread in the bottom and worked into the topsoil, along with peat moss, sand, compost, and fertilizer in the proportions we used for the vegetable garden. With our generous use of peat moss to lighten the clay subsoil, we needed a little lime, figuring that a pound of ground limestone counteracts the acidity of a bale of peat. When the soil was well worked, we left it rough, like the garden plot, until spring planting time.

Space is important. I started with a dozen raspberry crowns, six each of Latham and Indian Summer, in a twenty-foot strip along the fence. The bed is only two feet wide, and as the planting has developed to its full bearing capacity, I have had to be more and more ruthless in rooting out the lusty suckers by which the plants spread. Some have popped up six feet away among the pea vines; others crept into my neighbor's border, where they met with a delighted welcome. We now have the raspberry canes well in hand. A series of four stout posts six feet high mark the line beyond which they may not wander, and the posts are strung with heavy cord at eighteen-inch intervals so that the canes cannot flop across the path into the vegetable garden. I use cord instead of wire to pen in the raspberries, because it can easily be untied to readmit the canes that occasionally escape bounds and cannot be pushed back without danger of snapping off.

I have been fortunate in that my raspberries have so far been staunchly resistant to disease. I have occasionally had to cut out and burn a cane that wilted, and I take no chances with crumpled, distorted leaf tips, but destroy them at once. For prevention, I spray and dust the raspberries as I do the vegetable plot. Apart from these precautions, the raspberries demand relatively little attention. A good spring mulch of manure for the hungry roots and good soakings of water for the thirsty canes when the fruits are forming are about all they require.

Except thinning. It is a drastic business to keep a bramble patch from being a bramble patch in fact as well as name. In late summer, when we cut out the canes that have borne fruit, we also cut out new growth that is weak and spindly, allowing only eight or ten of the sturdiest canes to develop from each plant. These grow enormously, sometimes to eight or ten feet; I crop them off level with the tops of the posts in autumn so that they won't whip and break in winter winds. In spring we cut back any canes that have winterkilled and fill in scanty spots with suckers that have sprung up out of bounds. This method has had good results: the crop each year is heavy, since the fruitful canes have ample sun and room to grow, and we anticipate July with increasing eagerness.

And so do the birds. I have to do my raspberry picking early in the morning to foil them—even with a birdbath at hand, they prefer the water in the fruit and peck for it voraciously from berry to berry, choosing always, of course, the sweetest and ripest.

For the grapes, we allotted a bed three feet wide all along the side of the garage, to permit sufficient spread for the root system. We ordered year-old roots and set them eight feet apart, centered in the bed. That first summer, all that was needed for their support was a tomato stake; now, in their seventh year, they cover a trellis the length and height of the garage, and their yield is beginning to be bountiful.

Rhubarb, too, needs space. My three plants are in a bed

nine by three feet, and still their lush leaves hang over the path that separates them from the vegetables. Well-fed rhubarb is a lusty grower, and in spring the new shoots thrust up with the speed of Jack's beanstalk and the crinkly leaves unfold like fans overnight. I have found that it is easy to unsettle the crown of the plant if I am rough in pulling off stalks for cooking. I have learned to grasp the stalk near its base and give a quick outward twist of the wrist. By this method the stalk comes off with a clean break. For the maintenance of a sturdy plant it is important not to take more than a third of the stalks at any one time, and to let new leaves attain a good size before the next picking. I used to believe that the rhubarb season was over when the strangely exotic seed stalks began to rear up, but experience has taught me that this notion is an old wives' tale. We cut out the seed stalks when they appear, and keep right on cutting the tender, juicy rhubarb; it seldom grows stringy and tough before July.

My situation has been fortunate for these permanent plantings. It was possible to separate them by paths from the vegetable patch and thus they are not affected by the annual spading that the garden proper receives. The grapes, raspberries, and rhubarb do not require spading; in fact, they do best with only weeding and shallow cultivation—and of course fertilizing. I should reiterate the desirability of manure for this trio of back-yard specialties. All are heavy feeders, and manure is the ideal fertilizer to encourage heavy yield. My vegetable garden gets its mulch of manure in the fall, since part of my purpose is to lighten my clay soil. But the small fruits I manure in early spring. The rhubarb, especially, receives attention early. Before its growth starts, I inspect the rhubarb border for weeds, sprinkle it generously with manure—dried commercial manure if necessary—and stir up the soil a little. Spring rains and the vigor of the pie-plant do the rest; I am rewarded with luxuriant growth and fine flavor.

The patience of the gardener is tested when it comes to growing small fruits. Raspberries bear only a scanty crop the first and second years; one mustn't pull rhubarb the first season; my grapes were four years old before they bore at all. But the wait has been worth it, and now, except for the annual cultivating and mulching with manure and my struggles to grasp the Kniffen method of pruning grapevines, I have little trouble for the wealth I reap.

The proper pruning of grapevines is a mystery I have not yet been able to master. The first year it was simple enough: "At planting time, prune off all but the strongest cane. Cut that cane back to two buds." The second year, too, was comprehensible: "Remove all but the most vigorous single cane and leave it long enough to reach the first wire of the trellis." But the third year brought me to the Kniffen system, and I was lost. I read the manuals and tried to absorb the directions about fruiting canes, renewal spurs, and the number of canes and buds to leave or take off. It all seemed so clear as I read the text and consulted the diagrams. But when I went out to apply the directions to my own vines, they did not seem to be growing according to any pattern recognizable in the manual. I did the best I could, and the vines apparently flourished, but they bore no fruit, although this third year I had expected to pluck my first bunch of grapes.

The fourth season I took no chances. I reread the directions but called on a specialist in grape culture to demonstrate the Kniffen method for me. His was a masterly performance, done with quick, sure judgment, and that year I had my first grape harvest, small but delectable. I shall need another lesson or two before I can consider myself at all adept in the pruning of grapevines—it is still difficult for me to dare to cut back as drastically as my teacher does—but I feel more confident when February and pruning time roll around. I am developing an eye for the size of cane that is desirable for fruiting, neither too thick nor too willowy, and with buds fairly close together. And I practice a trick my demonstrator taught me, which is not mentioned in my manuals: rub off the buds that develop along the main trunk between the trellis wires so that the growing strength of the vines will be concentrated on the fruiting canes.

I had considered it a black mark against my intelligence that, armed with competent directions, I was unable to make a do-it-myself project of the Kniffen system of pruning, and I was diffident about asking to be shown how. But seasoned gardeners reassured me that many reasonably bright adults have the same trouble. So it is with no trace of defensiveness that I assert that getting a firsthand demonstration by an old hand with the pruning shears is the best way for the grape novice to learn the art of pruning. However, for those who prefer to try it the hard way as I did, I quote some of the briefest and clearest instructions of "Grapes: The Pruning Story"* I have ever come across. I disagree only with the qualifying clause in the

*Quoted with permission from "Grapes: The Pruning Story," by Montague Free. *Home Garden* magazine, November 1948.

first sentence, and might even have agreed with that if I had had these directions at hand when I made my first effort.

.... The four-cane Kniffen system of pruning and training is probably the most popular in the East and Middle West, and as it is also a simple one to follow, let us stick to it to avoid complications. First, it is desirable to learn the vocabulary, which should not be difficult since only five words are involved. The *shoot* is the growth which bears the fruit. This originates from the *cane* which grew the preceding year. This cane came either from a *renewal spur* (a cane cut back to two buds at pruning time) or directly from the trunk. The cane by the end of the growing season becomes the *arm*. The *trunk* is the more or less permanent vertical

Sketch 1   *Sketch 2*

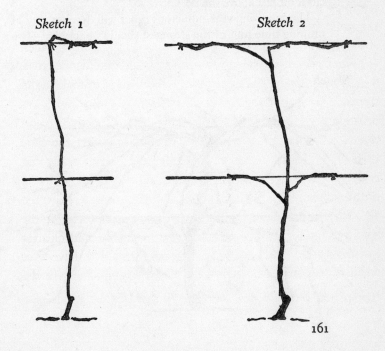

portion of the vine which carries all of the preceding categories.

A vine grown by the Kniffen system, then, has a trunk, four canes (later arms) and four spurs—all except the trunk being renewed annually. It is supported on a 2-wire trellis, the first wire being 30 inches from the ground, the second 30 inches above the first.

Let's start at the beginning. A one-year-old plant is set in the spring and cut back to two buds. If, during the season, canes in excess of 5 feet develop, the trellis can be erected and the strongest cane tied to the wires to form the trunk (*Sketch* 1). The rest are cut off and also the tip of the one tied to the trellis. (If growth has been poor, cut to two buds again, or tie the strongest shoot to the lower wire and cut it off just above the tie.)

The following year numerous canes will develop, and at pruning time four of the strongest should be selected—two

Sketch 3

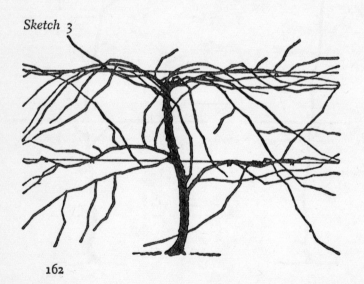

near the lower wire and two near the upper wire. These should be shortened, the topmost to five buds each, the lower to four buds (*Sketch 2*). All remaining canes are cut off.

The next year and subsequently the vine should look something like that in *Sketch 3*. Pruning will consist first of cutting out the arms (which have borne the fruiting shoots). Then select four strong canes to bear fruit during the coming season, and four canes each to be cut back to form spurs. Each of these spurs should have two buds which will produce canes from which will be chosen four canes to bear the fruiting shoots the following year (*Sketch 4*). The bearing canes should be shortened to ten to twelve buds (joints) on each of the top canes; eight to ten on each of the lower canes if the vine is very vigorous. If the vine is weak, pruning should be more severe, leaving only about six buds on each cane. . . .

Sketch 4

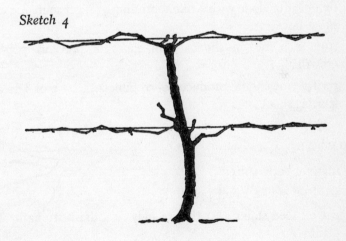

❨ JOTTINGS FROM THE GARDEN LOG

RASPBERRIES . . .

__ spring mulch of manure . . .

__ keep in bounds with stakes and heavy cord . . . grub out unwanted suckers . . .

__ water, water, water . . . fruiting time usually dry period of summer . . .

__ cut canes after fruiting . . . don't let the brambles be a bramble patch . . .

GRAPES . . .

__ prune on warm day . . . February thaw . . .

__ don't suffer alone with Kniffen pruning . . . get someone to *show* how . . .

__ fruit is borne on *shoots* from canes of previous year's growth . . .

__ thrifty vine should produce 40–50 bunches . . . 2 or 3 to a fruiting shoot . . .

RHUBARB . . .

__ manure early spring . . .

__ twist off stalks, don't pull . . .

__ cut off seed stalks . . . they're ugly . . . drain strength of plant . . .

17

CLEANUP
FOR
WINTER

In my pocket-sized kitchen garden the cleanup for winter is no arduous task reluctantly undertaken, but rather one I welcome for the comfortable sense of continuity it gives. As we enjoy the last of the late crops, I can look back and see how our patch of land has provided our household with vegetables and greens far superior to any we could have bought in market, and I know that we shall take delight in its bounty again next year. Now we prepare the earth for rest and replenishment. November marks the beginning of a period of repose both for the garden and for us who have worked for its fruition: we can soon stow away the spade and trowel with a clear conscience and take our ease by the fireside while the friendly snow falls.

Winter preparation of the garden is essentially simple, consisting chiefly of what the garden books prosaically call "good garden sanitation." Take it in easy stages and the final work can be accomplished some brisk November day in a few hours. During October and early November, as the last of the squash and beans, broccoli and tomatoes are finally harvested and killing frost blackens the plants, I make a practice of stripping off the dead stalks and vines at once. At the same time I remove the stakes and poles, which can be hosed off at once and later painted and bundled, to be stored away for another season. As we pull the last of the carrots and beets, the earth that is hidden by the lush foliage of summer crops is gradually exposed, black and crumbly, until only the garlic sprouts, the herb row, and the leeks still stand.

When these are bedded down, there remains the last rite of winter preparation: spading the garden. Some gardeners do not believe in fall spading; they prefer to sow the ground to winter rye, row by row as the harvest is completed, and then in spring dig under this nitrogenous green manure. My vegetable patch is too small—and too busy all through the fall—to make that worth while. Our practice is to turn over the soil to the depth of the spade, leaving the upturned clods rough and humpy to expose them to the beneficent breakup that comes with alternate freezing and thawing. No fertilizer goes on at this time, unless we are so lucky as to possess a few bushels of manure to broadcast over the lumpy ground. Faced with the choice between spring and fall manuring of the garden, my vote goes to fall in my soil of heavy clay base, though I would prefer to manure both spring and fall. It is almost impossible to over-fertilize a vegetable garden that is worked as heavily as mine is. Peat moss and the last of the grass cuttings can be spread on, too, to enrich further the supply of humus in the soil. This rough fall spading is something I am always grateful for in the following spring, for it makes the spring work-up much easier.

We shouldn't go into winter without a last thought for the compost piles. One of mine, started a year ago, is quietly disintegrating into rich humus. This year's pile has been building up all summer, so quickly that we have had to start a third pile with the heavy autumn leaf fall. As the garden was stripped, healthy green stuff went on the new pile; anything diseased or suspect we burned. The compost should really be forked over, dusted with Adco, covered with dirt, well wetted down, and the top made concave to catch winter rain and snow. My lazy method of leaving compost to its own devices omits the forking over, but I have been packing the pile down with Adco and earth and giving it an occasional watering as I added material to it. Now I give it a final tamping and a good watering. In spring we shall dig from beneath the old pile for compost to top-dress the garden.

When the garden is finally ready for winter, I gloat over it with great satisfaction, just as I do over the kitchen when it is scrubbed and shining after a particularly delicious meal. As the fragrance of food heartily enjoyed lingers in the kitchen, so in the garden the fresh smell of new-turned earth pervades the chill November air. It is good to look back over the summer season, counting success and failure, ruminating on the changes we shall make another year, much as we plan the improvement of a favorite dish or menu while we scour the kitchen after dinner.

In November, after the strenuous work of spading the garden, I am tired. Leaning on the spade, I survey my tight little vegetable kingdom. It has been a good year, I think with satisfaction, and now everything is done. Then I look down at the spade. Everything is not done; the tools are still to be cleaned and stored. I know myself too well to postpone the care of tools until some dull winter day; that day never comes. So the last chore of the garden—and a real chore it is—must be to clean and oil the trowel, the spade, the spading fork, the rake, and the cultivator. Only when this cleaning up is accomplished can I with good conscience take to the armchair by the fire.

And it is only a brief rest at that. To be shipshape for winter, the hoses must be drained and coiled and hung, the flowerpots and flats must be scrubbed. Oddments of fertilizer, insecticides, and fungicides must be inventoried and packed in cans, and I am wise if I bring in a basket of earth for repotting herbs and house plants. November should be paint-up month for self-respecting garden gear, though I can forgive myself if I let this job go until January or February. The cart and the wheelbarrow, gashed by spade and fork, should not properly be left to rust over the winter. They need touching up with rust remover and then a new gay coat of bright green. The trowel deserves a red handle, to make it easy to spot when mislaid somewhere along the garden rows.

And the stakes should be painted to prevent rotting. This was always the most irritating job of all, brushing over the rough wood, until I hit upon a dipping technique. We bought a three-foot length of pipe with a bore big enough to take the

inch-square stakes, and had it capped at one end so that we could pour paint into it. This device, gripped in the vise at the edge of the workbench, makes stake-painting easy: all we now have to do is to dip in one end of the stake for its coating of green paint—watch it! if the pipe is too full, the paint will overflow when the stake is inserted. Remove the stake, let it drip and dry, then dip the other half.

With the refurbishing of tools and stowing away of supplies, the garden year indeed winds up with a flourish. December is my month off. It is a relief to forget the garden for a while and concentrate on cooking for the holiday festivities. But those of us who pursue the goal of gardening for good eating are never at leisure for long. The first January thaw will stir in me the sublime but unsettling dream of the perfection of next year's garden, and I shall be haunting the front windows, watching for the postman to bring the first of the new spring catalogues.

⟦ JOTTINGS FROM THE GARDEN LOG

__ compost . . . check pile . . . one last packing and watering . . .

__ tools and equipment . . . clean . . . oil . . . or paint . . . store . . .

__ dried manure . . . fertilizer . . . store under cover outdoors if you value odor of cellar . . .

___ stake-painting . . . dip them like candles . . .

___ don't discard Christmas tree as rubbish . . . let it have one more useful function . . . cut off branches to protect herb row . . .

___ potted herbs nice Christmas remembrance for gourmet friends . . .

18

THE ARMCHAIR
AGAIN
—A TOTTING UP

As I suggested to begin with, the best way to plan a garden is
to settle comfortably in an armchair before dinner and dream
about food. And to conclude, I suggest that the best way to
close the gardening season is to settle comfortably in the armchair after dinner and tot up the pros and cons of what we have
grown. I like to do this to give myself a background against

which to do my dreaming about next year's gardening for good eating. Comparing Wade and Greencrop, relishing in retrospect the various virtues of Goldpak, Tendersweet, and Nantes, balancing the advantages and disadvantages—tastewise and gardenwise—of eggplant, zucchini, okra, cucumbers, broccoli, I can shape up my plan each year with a surer touch. Sipping the heady wine of anticipation, I correct the imagination's palate with the bread of experience.

The totting up is fruitful especially for planning the changes, the "let's trys," which make the small garden for gourmets a challenge and an excitement. The selections made in spring, the appraisals of midsummer, the plans for the future, all are rolled into one grand summing up, and we come full circle, ready to start again. For luckily nothing is final. That is one great charm of my kind of garden; there are always fresh adventures in the offing. Even in such a tight little plot I can make trial of some new vegetable or variety, to add to the zest of gardening and the satisfactions of the supper table. Over the years my fifteen by twenty-five vegetable patch has afforded me thumbnail sketches of many—by no means all—vegetables, both what I have grown in the past and what I now grow. These, with my notes on what I would like to grow, constitute my personal garden manual, handy reference for that delightful pastime, armchair gardening. They pull together the main points of what I have discussed discursively in this account of my ventures into gardening for gourmets.

ARTICHOKES The books are right. Not for this climate.

174

ASPARAGUS Alas, not for my present garden; another five feet and it would be feasible. Things to consider: short season crop and a space-waster; three years before it can stand heavy cutting. Greedy feeder; must have bed deeply prepared and richly fertilized with manure, both to begin with and annually thereafter. Easy of culture, few pests and diseases, good for fifteen years, pride of the home garden, first crop to welcome the new gardening season. Allow ten roots per family member —rust-resistant Mary Washington strain. Set roots 12 inches apart in trenches 5 to 8 inches deep (depending on heaviness of soil), 15 inches wide, and 24–30 inches apart. Fill soil in gradually; don't cut spears first year.

BEANS, Bush Snap Beans Summer stand-by. Greencrop slight edge over Wade. Fast-growing (50–60 days); heavy yield for space they take. Good for companion planting (with squash, eggplant) and succession planting (following early peas, beets, lettuce). Few enemies; rust only danger—don't harvest or work on when bean patch is wet. Plant May 1, 15, June 1; then August 1, 15, for fall crop. Plant 2 inches apart; spring sowing 1 inch deep, August sowings 2–3 inches deep; rows 15 inches apart. Beans like slight acidity; can use aluminum sulphate, 1 pound to 100 square feet. Do well in heavy, not too fertile soil. Packet plants 20 feet.

BEANS, Pole Snap Beans Kentucky Wonder, 64 days. No advantage over bush beans except space-saving and long season of yield. Plant late May. Need substantial poles; set poles 3 feet apart, plant 7 or 8 beans in circles around poles, 1 inch deep. Can interplant lettuce, radishes, scallions. Packet plants 3 poles, which is enough for me. Prefer stick to Greencrop.

BEANS, Lima Not even a "let's try" any more; too hard to shell. Fordhook 242 the standard variety, 74 days. Plant June 1; 3 or 4 seeds to a foot; thin to 8–10 inches. Rows 30 inches apart. Limas do better with plenty of air space. Packet sows 30 feet.

BEETS Burpee Redheart, Crosby's Egyptian, Detroit Dark Red. 55–65 days. Plant April 15, May 1, 15, and July 15 for late crop. Sow seed 2 to inch, ¼ inch deep, rows 10–12 inches apart. Thin to 3 inches when seedlings tall enough to eat as cooked greens—6–7 inches. Few pests. May need a little lime if leaves show up puny. (Try Ruby Queen, Bronze Medal 1958.) Packet sows 20 feet.

BROCCOLI Italian Green Sprouting standard variety. 70 days. A most satisfactory home-garden specialty; cut first heads when in tight bud; side heads develop in leaf axils; cut and come again until past frost. Buy plants; set out May 30, 15 inches apart; rows 2 feet apart. Watch for cabbage worms, aphids, otherwise few pests, no diseases. If ever try from seed, 1 packet ample—produces 200 plants.

CABBAGE Golden Acre. Quick-maturing (62 days); small, crisp, tender heads. A fill-in, late-season crop. Sow a couple of feet to seed June 1 for seedlings to transplant in August. Sow seeds 1 inch apart in shallow furrow, cover ¼ inch. Thin to 2 inches apart; transplant when 6 inches high. Will spread to 18 inches. Worth putting on a cardboard collar to protect from cabbage maggot; otherwise don't bother to try to identify all worms and bugs that flock to young cabbage leaves, just keep at it with all-purpose insecticide. Packet produces 250 plants, but a dozen heads are all I want. Let's try Cabbage Red Acre for a change of flavor and stunning leaves, iridescent red and green. Wonderful cooked with apple and onion, red wine and grape jelly.

CABBAGE, *Chinese Cabbage*   A "let's try" late crop. No luck with Chihli, try Michihli. 80 days. A fill-in crop. Plant July 15 to August 1 wherever bare space in garden; goes to seed if planted too early. Plant seed 3 or 4 to the foot, 1 inch deep; thin to 12–18 inches. Packet sows 40 feet.

CARROTS   Have tried Sweetheart, Oxheart, Goldpak, Tendersweet, Nantes Half-long. Last two are my choice. 70–75 days. No lumpy soil for carrots, and they like slight acidity (1 pound aluminum sulphate per 100 square feet if needed). Plant April 15, May 10, June 1. Won't do well in hot months but can plant August 1, 15, for fall crop lasting well into November. Plant 3–4 seeds to inch, barely cover; rows 10–12 inches apart. Thin to 1 inch apart, then to 3 apart when thinnings are of a size to eat as fingerlings. No pests or diseases, but slugs will nibble. Packet plants 30 feet.

CHARD Burpee Rhubarb Chard. Really a cut-and-come-again version of beet greens, dark green leaf with ruby-red midrib. Fast grower (60 days) and, so long as the growing tip is unmolested, produces right up to killing frost. Trick is to tear off and discard all old leaves; clip for cooking those that are 6–8 inches long. Plant May 1; 2–3 seeds to the inch; cover ¼ inch; thin to 4 inches apart; between rows, 15 inches. Packet sows 15 feet; plenty for a household that likes its cooked greens only once a month. Two seasons of chard and we wanted a change.

CORN On the docket for next season! Space-waster and short season of yield, but where else than from the home garden can one be sure of corn as it should be: 20 minutes, stalk to table? Many choice varieties; can plant early, mid-season, and late varieties all at once, or succession sowings of one variety. For my garden, start with North Star (67 days), Wonderful (81 days), Golden Harvest (84 days); or three plantings of Golden Midget Hybrid (68 days). Also recommended by friends: Spancross (71 days), Golden Beauty (73 days), Iochief (89 days). Plant April 25; 3–4 kernels to the foot, 1 inch deep; thin to 10–12 inches. Rows 2–2½ feet apart. No single rows of corn; always plant in blocks of two or more rows for proper pollination. Spray for borers; pick off smut balls. Expect 2–3 ears per stalk. Packet plants 100 feet.

CUCUMBERS Burpee Hybrid (60 days); Smoothie (66 days). Space-waster and not too dependable, but a "must" in my garden. Requires about 4 feet square as usually grown, but takes less when planted near something it can climb on—tomatoes, broccoli, fence, or trellis. Start seed in jiffy pots early May; transplant Memorial Day to two "hills"—flowerpots filled with manure sunk in soil—ringed with 6–7 seedlings; thin to four sturdiest plants before they start to vine. At same time, start second planting in two other hills with same system—7–8 seeds planted ½ inch deep in circle around manure-filled sunken pots. Spray for cucumber beetle. Male and female flowers borne on same vine; females will ripen into cucumbers, males will wither and fall off. Packet will plant four hills; seeds keep, can be used a second year.

EGGPLANT BLACK BEAUTY, 80 days   Packet will provide 100 plants, but I prefer to buy 3 seedlings, set out May 30th. Easy culture; expect 3–4 mature eggplants from each bush.

FINOCCHIO   Called Florence Fennel in catalogues (80–90 days). Technically an herb; a good "let's try" for anise flavor and celery-like texture. Feathery leaves delectable in omelet. Sow in May or June, rich soil; seeds 1 inch apart, ½ inch deep. Thin to 2 inches; then when 6 inches tall, thin again to 12–18 inches apart, using thinnings for relish tray, like scallions. Watch facial expressions of surprise at unexpected flavor. When plants are half grown and bulbs begin to swell, hill up plants to blanch. Packet sows more footage than anyone in right mind wants.

GARLIC Wouldn't develop for me until planted in September instead of spring. ¼ pound of mother bulbs more than ample; share with friend. Select spot at edge of garden where spring spading won't interfere. Mine happy at one end of cucumber row. Flake bulbs into separate cloves; plant 3–4 inches deep, 4 inches apart; rows 12 inches apart. No special care except weed and mulch with manure late fall. Harvest when tops break over, about mid-July. Tie tops in clumps, hang up to dry in airy place. Don't let bulbs freeze.

HERBS 1 packet of each more than enough. Except as noted, plant all seeds about May 15; 3–4 to the inch (for more even distribution of fine seeds, mix with dry sand). Barely cover. Thinnings have flavor when seedlings 2–3 inches tall; pull sprigs as needed; otherwise leave dense.

— S W E E T   B A S I L   Plants grow 2–2½ feet high, so place at north end of herb row. Thin to stand 12 inches apart, using thinnings for seasoning. Pinch out tip to force compact bush. Snip off single leaves or branch tips as needed. Special affinity: tomatoes, vinegar.

__ CHERVIL Mild flavor of anise. Grows like parsley. Seldom listed in catalogues; try specialty seed shops or herb farms. Likes slight shade, preferably of taller plants. Delicate root system; doesn't transplant well. Don't pull seedlings; nip off at ground level to thin to 2 inches. Seeds keep for three years. French use it in everything from soup to salad. Special affinity: omelet, broiled fish.

__ CHIVES A must for all gardens. Can be set out any time soil is workable. Most self-sufficient herb. One pot from grocer's will spread a foot across in a year or two. No pests, no diseases. Flowers pretty in arrangements—like blue clover. Cut flower stalks to ground. If shoots grow tall and flop, give butch haircut to 4 inches and shot in arm of fertilizer.

__ DILL Worth a whole row to itself. Plant April 15, May 10, 30, in row separate from other herbs—it grows 3 feet tall. Doesn't transplant well. Thin to 3, then to 6 inches; thinnings have flavor when seedlings are 5–8 inches tall. Self-sows vigorously and plants are much sturdier; let these volunteers mature even if it gives garden a rakish air. Special affinity: cucumbers, potatoes, tomatoes, fish.

__ MARJORAM Sweet marjoram most flavorsome for cooking. Slow to germinate. Makes upright little bush about 8 inches tall. Leave dense, pulling sprigs as needed until plants are 2 inches apart. Special affinity: chicken stuffing, sausage meat, cheese.

__MINT__ Of 30-odd native species, I have two: spearmint and lemon mint. Mint such a wanderer must be planted apart from garden, preferably penned in by metal tub with bottom knocked out. Likes moist shade. In very early spring, chop mint bed deeply with spade to cut root runners; new shoots will spring up from cut root ends, making a dense mat. Keep tops cut back even if not used; plants may die down if flower stalks are allowed to go to seed. Don't use manure. Special affinity: juleps. In my household, never in peas or with lamb.

__PARSLEY__ Prefer plain for flavor over curly for garnish. Plant April 15. Slow to germinate. A biennial, but I prefer to treat as annual, keeping over 1 plant to use until new seedlings ready in spring. Thin to 2 inches apart; cutting leaves back encourages thick growth. Pot up for house, or winter over with protection of basket filled with leaves. Can cut even in January. Special affinity: anything except dessert.

__ROSEMARY__ A must in my garden for biscuits and to rub on roast lamb. Very slow to germinate, sometimes more than 3 weeks. Treat as annual or it may grow 5 feet high, if roots don't freeze. In one season, makes a compact, spiny little bush 6 or 7 inches high. Thin plants to 5 inches apart; snip branch tips sparingly. Likes a taste of lime now and then. Pot up for house, or winter over like parsley.

__SUMMER SAVORY__ A "let's try" for several seasons, but not too satisfactory in small gardens because weak-stemmed and sprawly. Grows 18 inches high; thin plants to 6 inches. Nice in salad, stuffing, and stew.

__TARRAGON Only if you like taste of anise. Beg a root cutting from friend; doesn't set seed. Rather finicky herb; doesn't like cold wet feet, does like rich soil and partial shade. Spready little plant, can grow to 18 inches high. Tends to winterkill unless well mulched with leaves and uncovered very gradually in spring. Special affinity: vinegar, chicken, salad, broiled fish.

__THYME Bushy plant with miniature leaves; spreads in a mat about a foot high. If treated as perennial, thin to 6 inches; keep plants clipped back or stems become woody. Like rosemary, thyme likes a little lime in the soil. Special affinity: chowders, stuffing, meat sauces.

KALE Dwarf Blue Curled (55 days). A "let's try" for one year only. However, quick-growing and very hardy, not attractive to pests. Good as late crop; planted 2 months before frost, can be harvested as late as December. Sow seed August 1–15; 1 or 2 seeds to the inch; cover ½ inch. Thin or transplant to stand 12 inches apart; rows 18 inches apart. Packet plants 30 feet.

LEEKS One of my most important musts. Sweet and mild onion flavor. London Flag (130 days). Long season, husky vegetable. Sow seed April 15 in V-shaped furrow 6 inches deep; space seeds 3–4 to the inch; barely cover. Let soil seep into furrow as seedlings sprout—spring rains will attend to this. Thin to 3 inches. Leeks tend to their own business as they grow and thicken; no pests or diseases. Only care needed: hill up to blanch stalks in late fall. Leave in ground over winter, protected with leaves fenced in with boards. Can be dug as needed even in sub-zero weather. Packet sows 20 feet.

LETTUCE Hard to choose among Salad Bowl (48 days), Matchless (60 days), Bibb (58 days), Oakleaf (45 days), and Great Lakes (80 days). Plant in short stretches every three weeks starting April 1. Cold-weather fan, no use sowing after June 1 until August 15 for fall crop. Oakleaf, Bibb good for late crop. Plant 3–4 seeds to the inch, broadcast in furrow 3 inches wide; barely cover; rows 12 inches apart. Thin to 3 inches apart, then to 6, then to 10 for mature plants. Use thinnings in salad. Stretch season by cutting leaves from base of mature plants, rather than pulling entire head. Packet sows 40 feet.

LETTUCE, ROMAINE (COS) Paris White (72 days). Like Great Lakes, slower in growth than my other lettuce choices. Tried it for three seasons; a disappointing crop—it never would head up thickly for me. Planting, same as other lettuces; thin to 8 inches apart. Packet sows 40 feet.

OKRA Clemson Spineless (56 days). Beautiful velvety white flowers; pods develop almost overnight after flower drops off. Not practical for my size of garden; would need a dozen plants for worth-while crop; other things we like better in the space okra would require. Sow seed 3 or 4 to a foot, cover ¼ inch; rows 18 inches apart. Thin to 15 inches. Easy culture, no special enemies. Pick pods very young and tender; old pods are woody and good only for compost. Packet sows 15 feet.

184

ONION   I prefer to buy white onion sets and make successive sowings starting April 15, until bulbs start to sprout in the bag. Poke bulblets 1 inch deep into soil, almost touching. Thin to 1 inch, then to 3, using intervening bulbs as scallions. Onions are mature when tops break over and tips turn brown. No luck with my one attempt to raise onions from seed; said to be tricky and often not successful unless sown very early. Try Sweet Spanish (115 days) planted along with peas April 1. Sow seed 15 to the foot, ½ inch deep; rows 12 inches apart. Thin to 3 inches as with sets. Packet sows 25 feet.

PEAS   Wando (67 days) first choice in my climate, where we expect sudden hot spells in June–July. Little Marvel, Greater Progress (62 days) second choices, with advantage that they have dwarf vines (18 inches) as against Wando (30 inches). Must plant as early as ground is workable (March 17 to April 1 in my climate). Safe to make second planting April 15, even May 1. Plant seeds 1 inch apart, 1 inch deep—poke into earth and pat firm. Make double rows 4 inches apart; between double rows, 2–2½ feet. No need to thin. Fill in gaps of 2 or more inches if seeds fail to germinate. Can interplant peas with tomatoes, squash, or follow peas with snap beans. Packet sows 15 feet; 1 pound, 100 feet.

PEPPERS, green California Wonder, 76 days.   Packet provides 75 plants, but I buy seedlings and set out May 30. No pests, no diseases. Four plants enough for our household. Peppers never give me much of a crop before September, but harvest them right up to frost.

RADISHES   Always thought no one could go wrong on radishes, but my next-door neighbor claimed his radish roots were never anything but strings. Last summer he used my seed, soil, and planting schedule; sure enough, nothing but strings. Mine did valiantly. Cherry Belle (24 days), Champion (28 days), White Icicle (30 days). Make successive sowings two weeks apart starting April 1; 3 or 4 seeds to the inch, ¼ inch deep; thin to 2 inches. Resow August for fall crop. Can tuck in anywhere—between bean rows, beside broccoli. No pests, no diseases. Packet sows 20 feet. Let's try Black Spanish (55 days) for fall crop; plant in August.

SQUASH   Zucchini Black Beauty (60 days). Start seeds ½ inch deep in jiffy pots early in May; transplant to garden May 30. Mature plants will take up 3 feet square. Bugs love squash leaves; keep sprayed. Don't expect fruit from every flower—male flowers will drop off. Keep picking and the vines will keep producing. Frost-tender—harvest before heavy frost. Packet plants 8–10 hills.

TOMATOES   Marglobe (80 days), Rutgers (82 days), Jubilee (yellow, 80 days), Red Cherry (72 days). Set stakes before plants. Buy stocky plants, preferably pot-grown; set out May 30. Vines grow fast; keep tied to stakes with Twistems. Watch for axillary suckers; pinch out all except one or two of the first to sprout. Blossoms don't set fruit well when night temperature is below 59 or above 68; if temperature unfavorable, spray with fruit-setting hormone. Keep an eye out for tomato hornworm. Before heavy frost, pick fruit to ripen in house. If try from seed, start 10 weeks before date of last frost. Packets usually contain 50 seeds.

TURNIPS Purple Top White Globe (58 days). No luck with early crop—plant August 1–15. Sow seeds 1 inch apart, 12 inches between rows. Thin to 4 inches. Not popular with insects or grubs, nor too popular with me. Packet sows 50 feet.

19

WINTER
WONDERLAND

On the fifteenth of last March I proudly ate the first radish I had ever grown indoors under lights—a small but very respectable Cherry Belle with the good old hot radish tang. This event marked the first success of some experimentation I had undertaken to see whether a casual lover of good eating, like myself, would find it worth while to grow a few herbs and greens from seed for winter use. I am happy to report, for the benefit of herb lovers who have been too long in city pent, that such a scheme is entirely feasible and need not be elaborate.

All winter I have been able to cut marjoram, thyme, rosemary, basil, and parsley for the refreshment of winter salads, soups, and stews. I took a fling on the radishes and some oakleaf lettuce just for the fun of it, and they too flourished, albeit in miniature: my radishes run a little more than half an inch in diameter, and the rosettes of the oakleaf lettuce spread about eight inches across. Hardly a crop, but superb as a conversation piece.

One learns from mistakes. My first effort was directed to window-sill gardening, with a window box installed in my workroom by my desk. I used loam from my garden, followed my usual practice in sowing the seeds of herbs, lettuce, and radishes, and kept the box covered with polyethylene film to preserve moisture. The seeds sprouted nicely and I had a little regiment of seedlings all slanting toward the sun at exactly the same angle, as if on dress parade. But alas, one morning my window garden looked like a battlefield strewn with dead. Nearly all my seedlings had toppled over with damping off; the luck I have always enjoyed in outdoor gardening did not follow me into the house. Severest loss was among the lettuces and radishes; the basil was not much affected—the other herbs had not yet germinated at the time. This taught me my first lesson about indoor gardening: the planting medium must be sterile.

Next I found out about temperature. The surviving seedlings shot up with unseemly haste and in their reach for light grew gangling and weak-stemmed. The little first leaves of the lettuces had long, spindly midriffs that rounded out into leaf only at the tips—their general contour was that of a straight-handled teaspoon. The radishes had three inches of stem before putting forth true leaves. The basil had as much as four inches of stem between pairs of leaves; the other herbs were similarly elongated. This was no new experience for me; as I have mentioned, the herbs I pot up for winter tend to grow weak and leggy in the warmth of the kitchen window. Legginess is disappointing enough in an established plant, but in young seedlings it is disastrous. And these seedlings, as I found out when I began to take temperature readings, were living in a hothouse. Protected by the polyethylene film, which keeps in moisture but also lets plants breathe, their atmosphere was around seventy degrees even at night and, when the sun shone, in the high eighties. The discovery led me to keep the window open a crack day and night, and this corrected the difficulty. Under the film, night readings fell to fifty degrees, which is ideal for seedlings; by day, the temperature rose to sixty or thereabouts, and on sunny days to about seventy-five. Thus I learned the importance of coolness for the successful growth of seedlings: the first batch stopped stretching, and the second batch, now just sprouted, grew far more normally.

But there was still the problem of insufficient light, which is of course the major factor in spindly growth. Short daylight hours, sunless winter days—how could the seedlings prosper, craving as they do the long, sunny days of May and June? The radishes and lettuce never reached edible proportions in the window box; the herbs were usable, but hardly satisfactory as plants. And so I was led to explore the art of raising herbs from seed under artificial light.

This hobby is a recent development among amateur horti-culturists, and the way is apparently being paved by the flower lovers, especially the African-violet enthusiasts. The only two books that I know of which cover this fascinating field of ex-periment are *Growing Plants Under Artificial Light*, by Peggie Schulz (Barrows), and *Gardening Indoors Under Lights*, by Frederick and Jacqueline Kranz (Viking); both books concen-trate on flowers and house plants and have relatively little to say about vegetables, herbs, and greens, although the Kranzes do have a chapter on vegetables, and Mrs. Schulz has a short section on salad crops and herbs. Both, however, are gold mines of information about the techniques of the art, and Mrs. Schulz, particularly, is full of ideas about adapting furniture and con-verting odd corners into miniature greenhouses. The appetite of the gourmet gardener is whetted by the vistas these authors open up.

It happens that Mrs. Schulz's ideas on uses for white ele-phants set me off hunting something from which to contrive a plant box. And right in my own workroom was the perfect white elephant: a long, narrow blanket box left over from my effi-ciency-apartment days, now in use as a low shelf for the stacks of garden magazines, government pamphlets, and agricultural reports I keep handy to my desk for reference. This box is a three-sided affair. It was designed to be placed with its open side against the wall; its dimensions were fifty-six inches in length, in depth ten inches, and in height twenty-one inches. The top was hinged for easy packing of blankets and pillows.

LIGHT SWITCH

Turn it around, and there is a completely practicable plant box.

Do-it-yourself wizards could easily complete the transformation; I had to call for help. We painted the inside of the box white, to get as much reflection as possible, installed two four-foot fluorescent daylight lamps and a switch, and I was in business. I stationed the plant box in front of the window where my first and second batches of seedlings were still struggling along in the window box, so that the crack of air could be maintained for coolness. The window box itself I transferred to the plant box, setting it on two upturned flowerpots to bring the seedlings close to the lights.

This makeshift arrangement has proved very practical: by using pots of varying heights (bricks—or even stacks of old magazines—would do as well) I can keep the window box and the several pans of seedlings I have since started at whatever distance from the light seems to promote their optimum growth. A length of polyethylene film thrown over the box hangs down like a curtain and keeps the interior properly humid. Daily watering of the soil, plus misting of leaves with a rubber bulb spray, is a necessity; the plants thrive when the polyethylene curtain begins to bead with moisture. Once or twice a fuzzy white mold has appeared on the stems of seedlings at soil surface; I have only to throw back the curtain to let the box dry out a little, and that damage is undone.

It took only a few days for the window-box seedlings to respond to their new environment. The lettuce from the first sowing remained puny, but it straightened up from its sidewise slant and took on a healthy green. Marjoram, thyme, rosemary, and parsley, slow growers that they are, began to be the sturdy little plants one expects them to be. The basil developed new stem-strength and, while still twisted and curved, put out fresh leaves and side branches and grew right up to the lights. At that point I cut off the tops to use with baked tomatoes and was pleased to find that the lower branches then spread and grew. The radish seedlings plumped up, and I knew that my crop of ten Cherry Belles was assured.

I was enchanted by the energy my new little plants displayed when afforded long stretches of "daylight." I keep them at their business of growing for a good sixteen hours out of the twenty-four—as long as a day in June—by flipping on the lights of the plant box upon awakening and turning them off the last thing at night. Radishes were of edible size in five weeks on the dot; the miniature heads of the lettuces had two dozen leaves in seven weeks; in six weeks the seedling herbs were four inches high and beginning to put forth side shoots.

Encouraged by the success of my venture with the window box under lights—even with the damping off I had a dozen Cherry Belles, half a dozen lettuces, and more herbs than I could conveniently pot up individually—I did a little experimenting with planting media. I have had good success both with sphagnum moss and vermiculite. My preference has settled upon the latter: both are safely sterile, but vermiculite holds moisture better under the cool warmth of the fluorescent lamps, and the damp particles which adhere to the rootlets, come time to transplant to soil, conserve moisture where needed, so that growth is not checked in the process of transplanting. Since neither sphagnum moss nor vermiculite contains any nutrients, it is necessary to keep the seedlings well fed with liquid fertilizer (I used the same fish-oil emulsion that I use on my African violets) from the moment they sprout. I water them with fertilizer twice a week while they are in vermiculite; when they are transferred to potting soil, a weekly feeding keeps them flourishing.

I don't advise a window box for gardening under lights; I just happened to start with one. The dirt-filled box is heavy to shift, is much deeper than necessary, and is too big to allow flexible handling of seedlings in various stages of development. It is far more satisfactory to start seed in bulb pans, shallow perforated composition trays, jiffy pots, or plant bands. When the seedlings sprout and are big enough to handle, they can be transferred to two-inch, then to three- or four-inch pots.

There are advantages to pots and pans other than ease of handling. With pots, for example, I can have herbs handy in the kitchen. To keep myself so supplied with a minimum of effort, I have worked out a plan of alternation and a starting system which eliminates one step of transplanting. I start with jiffy pots, half fill them with soil, and put a scant inch of vermiculite on top. I scatter a few seeds of, say, marjoram on the vermiculite, sprinkle a little more vermiculite over the seeds, and give the pots a good but very gentle watering. The seeds sprout and grow with no danger of damping off, and as the roots lengthen, they reach down into the soil and are nourished. When the seedlings are well up, I pinch out all but four and sink the jiffy pot in a soil-packed four-inch flowerpot. As the plants develop, their roots push right through the jiffy pot, and it in turn gradually disintegrates. Two pots of marjoram keep me going all winter: one stays in the plant box, the other goes down to the kitchen to fulfill its flavorsome function. After a month or so of culinary snipping, I take the kitchen marjoram up to the plant box to recuperate—it hasn't suffered at all; in fact, it has benefited from the change to incandescent lighting —and the second pot takes its turn with the cook.

Then there is the matter of light intensity. My seedling greens and herbs do best when they are so placed as almost to touch the lights; a trayful of pots with plantlets of the same height is easy to shift up or down as growth proceeds. The radishes—they do well planted in a bulb pan, thinned to ten or twelve radishes to an eight-inch pan—matured nicely two or three inches below the lights. An established pot of rosemary, brought in from the garden in September, took on new life, vigor, and color when I placed it so that the top leaves were ten inches below the lights, but it really began to flourish when I moved it up to within four inches.

I do not pretend to understand the mysteries of foot candles and light rays, and fortunately I don't need to: my herbs have done well enough to prove that an unashamed dilettante can have fresh herbs in winter as well as in summer, and the lettuce and radishes have been fun, to boot.

Indoor gardening under lights has immense possibilities for the really avid gardener. For those of scientific bent, it can be a hobby as challenging as hi-fi or photography—and considerably less expensive, although elaborate arrangements are decidedly not cheap. All the intricacies of plant propagation are there to explore: the exact light intensity that is best for this or that particular seedling or cutting; the optimum time under lights; the best combination of fluorescent and incandescent lighting; the most desirable degrees of humidity and temperature; and the relation of each of these factors to all the rest. There are endless elaborations upon my rudimentary plant box to egg the enthusiast on: floral carts, greenhouses in the cellar or the hall closet, plant cases, terrariums, lighted shadow boxes. And there are gadgets to delight the addict: light meters, automatic timers, humidity regulators. My lazy temperament does not lead me in these directions; I am content to be casual and opportunistic in indoor as in back-yard gardening—so long as I can achieve my goal of good eating.

I can see enticements for gourmet gardeners, however, in a setup of fluorescent lights as simple as mine. If I had a kitchen or pantry cupboard fifty-two inches long, for example, I could install the standard four-foot lights under the cupboard and devote the back of the counter to herb culture. There they would be easy to tend as I went about my kitchen work and handier for use than the herb row in the vegetable garden. How delightful, too, to be able to enjoy the scent of herbs as one prepares supper, to be able to pluck and crush a leaf of thyme and sniff its fragrance as one stands by the stove stirring a sauce or stew.

It is always a pleasure to herb lovers to be able to make gifts of little pots of garden-grown herbs; I frequently pot up rosemary, marjoram, or thyme for friends at the end of the gardening season. With my plant box, I shall now have the opportunity to give herbs—gay in tiny plastic pots—as Christmas remembrances to apartment-dwelling friends. And not only for Christmas: birthdays, New Year, Easter—or as "thank you" for a pleasant evening. It is fun, too, to tie to the pot a favorite recipe which calls for the particular herb.

Finally, to those who, like myself, have small gardens and no spot in the house adapted to starting vegetable seedlings indoors, a plant box can have many advantages. It is of course cheaper to buy seed packets than seedling plants. Tomatoes, cucumbers, eggplant, squash, peppers, cabbage can be sown indoors about six weeks before setting-out time, and one can also get a head start on the herb row. One can try off-beat varieties that are new, or not popular enough to be available in small lots to the home gardener. It was, for example, some years after Burpee brought out its tomato Big Boy before it could be bought locally in our garden shops; I have still to find a nurseryman who will sell me the three plants I would need to try out the tomato Long Red, which has been highly recommended for this area. Other advantages will appear, I am sure, as I try other ways of using the plant box.

In this book I have made much of the satisfactions of small-scale gardening for good eating: the utter deliciousness of fresh, home-grown vegetables; the freedom from the tyranny of the bumper crop; the fun of trying something new when failure needn't be catastrophe; the sweet savor of success when some bypath leads to greater enjoyment of the dinner hour. My adventure with herbs under lights confirms that thesis and adds a new point. I started the experiment in pity for friends who wistfully said, "I love fresh herbs, I've tried to keep them going in my apartment, but they always die. How does one keep them alive through the winter?" The answer is that they can be kept alive, given a suitable white elephant, $14.95 for lighting equipment, two yards of polyethylene film, a bag of vermiculite and a peck of good garden loam, a bottle of fish-oil emulsion, such oddments as teaspoons, bulb water sprays and assorted pans and flowerpots, eighty-three cents a month on the electric bill, and a modicum of patience and tender, loving care. They can even be started from scratch, with seed.

In demonstrating this point, I have gained a personal dividend: I, too, whose herbs have languished in winter, can have them fresh and succulent while the snow swirls under dark skies—and without the undue effort which to me would be anathema. That's what I like about gardening for good eating. Adventure waits by the garden path for those of us who allow the taste for good food to lead us on.

20

COME
INTO
THE KITCHEN

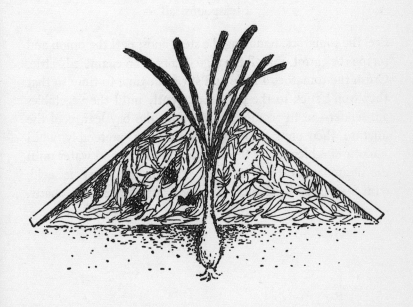

SPICED
TOMATO
JUICE

2 quarts (about 10) dead-ripe tomatoes
1 small onion
1 carrot
2 stalks celery with leaves
3 sprigs parsley
½ green pepper
1 bay leaf
1 teaspoon peppercorns
4 cloves
4 allspice
1 teaspoon Worcestershire sauce
2 slices lemon
2 teaspoons salt

Peel the tomatoes, removing the stem ends; peel the onion and scrape the carrot. Put all the ingredients in an enameled kettle. Crush the tomatoes a little and stir from time to time so that they won't stick to the pot. Cook gently until the vegetables are tender—20 to 30 minutes. Remove the bay leaf, cool the mixture, then press through a food mill or, preferably, whirl smooth in a blender. If the juice is very thick, add water until the desired consistency is reached. Chill and serve ice-cold, with a sprig of basil tucked in the glass. Makes 1½ quarts.

RUSSIAN
BORTSCH

18 to 20 medium-sized beets, peeled and
  sliced thin
¾ cup sliced onion, packed down
1 tablespoon salt
4 tablespoons sugar
4 tablespoons lemon juice
1 cup sour cream

Put 2 quarts of cold water in a soup kettle; add 2 teaspoonfuls of the salt and the beets and onion. Let them steep for an hour, then simmer for 1½ hours. Strain out the liquid, discarding the beets and onion, and prepare to season the soup. Start with less than the recommended quantities of salt, sugar, and lemon juice, then taste. Add a little more of each, tasting as you go, until the flavor is right for your palate. Bortsch may be served hot or cold. In either case, pass sour cream to garnish the bowl. You may float thin slices of cucumber in chilled bortsch for a summer soup. Russians like to serve cold bortsch with hot boiled potatoes, which they mash in the soup bowl. Makes about 2 quarts.

COLD
BROCCOLI
SOUP

> 4 to 6 stalks broccoli (or 1 package, frozen)
> 1½ cups chicken broth
> 2 slices onion, chopped
> ⅛ teaspoon chili powder
> ½ teaspoon salt
> ¼ teaspoon fresh-ground pepper
> 1 cup heavy cream

Cook the broccoli rapidly in boiling, salted water until just tender and still bright green. Put it in the blender with all other ingredients. Blend for 1 minute, then chill. Makes 4 servings.

CORN-CURRY SOUP*

2 cups corn, either scraped fresh, or
cream-style canned
1 tablespoon finely minced onion
½ cup milk
½ teaspoon salt
¼ teaspoon white pepper
½ teaspoon curry powder
1 cup cream
1 tablespoon butter
Paprika

Add corn, onion, salt, and pepper to the milk, simmer gently
for 10 minutes, then whirl in a blender or strain, mashing all
corn grains. Stir in the curry, cream, and butter. Heat, but do
not boil. Sprinkle with paprika before serving. Makes 4 servings.

*Recipes marked with asterisk are used with permission from the author's
Cooking by the Garden Calendar, Doubleday & Co., New York, 1955.

MINESTRA*

THE BASIC SOUP	4 carrots
	4 potatoes
	2-inch wedge of cabbage
	1 clove garlic
	1 onion
	4 stalks celery with leaves
	1 leek
	1 small bunch parsley
	2 teaspoons salt
	1 can kidney beans
	2 tomatoes (or ½ can)
	1 teaspoon chopped basil
	1 tablespoon olive oil
	½ teaspoon pepper
	Grated Parmesan or Romano cheese

OPTIONAL ADDITIONS	Handful of spinach
	1 cup peas or green beans
	Flowerets of broccoli or cauliflower
	Rice, barley, spaghetti, or noodles
	Pinch of marjoram or rosemary
	Thin-sliced frankfurter or shredded ham

Put 2 quarts of cold water in a large kettle; add the salt and the carrots, potatoes, cabbage, and garlic. These go in whole. Chop coarsely the onion, celery, leek, and parsley. Add these; boil up the soup and let it simmer for 1 hour. Lift out the whole vegetables and mash them with a fork or wire potato masher, then return them to the soup. Add the remaining ingredients (except the cheese) and simmer the soup for another hour. When served, pass the grated cheese to sprinkle on top. A combination of the suggested additional ingredients may be added, either at the time of making the soup or to vary it thereafter. Makes about 3 quarts.

FRENCH
ONION SOUP*

4 medium onions
3 tablespoons butter or drippings
4 cups beef stock†
Salt
Pepper
Thick slices toasted dry French bread
Grated Parmesan or Romano cheese

Shave the onions into the butter in a heavy skillet and brown them thoroughly; some may be allowed to fry crisp. Add the stock and simmer for ½ hour. Taste for seasoning, and add salt and pepper as needed. Have the toast hot; lay slices in a heated tureen or individual bowls and sprinkle them generously with grated cheese. Pour on the boiling soup to melt the cheese. Sprinkle more cheese on each bowlful when served. Makes about 1 quart.

†If homemade beef stock is not at hand, canned consommé may be substituted, but boil it up with carrot, celery, parsley, a sliver of garlic, and a piece of bay leaf to enrich the flavor. Strain out these vegetables before pouring it on the onions.

CRÉME
VICHYSSOISE

½ cup chopped onions
2 cups chopped leeks (white part only)
¼ cup melted butter
2 cups raw diced potatoes
1 quart chicken stock
Salt and white pepper
1 cup light cream
2 tablespoons chopped chives

Sauté the onions and leeks in the butter until they are transparent—about 20 minutes. Add the potatoes and stock, with salt to taste if needed, and pepper. When the potatoes are soft (10 to 15 minutes), press through a fine sieve, food mill, or whirl in a blender while hot. If the soup is to be served hot, return it to the stove, add the cream, and heat thoroughly without allowing it to boil. Sprinkle chives on top.

For cold vichyssoise, chill the soup thoroughly before adding the cream and the chive topping. Add cream only to the portion likely to be eaten at one time. The cream tends to sour quickly even when the soup is kept on ice; without the cream, it will keep for several days in the refrigerator. Makes about 2 quarts.

HUNGARIAN CHICKEN POT*

> 4 pounds backs and necks of chicken
> 4 pounds chicken wings
> 2 pounds chicken giblets
> ¼ cup chopped parsley
> 2 big onions
> 2 cloves garlic
> 3 stalks celery
> ½ cup Scotch barley
> 1 cup chopped celery
> 1 can kidney beans
> 4 large tomatoes (or 1 can)
> 2 spinach plants, broken raw (¼ lb.)
> 1 bay leaf
> 8 peppercorns
> 4 cloves
> 6 allspice
> 1 teaspoon chopped marjoram (½ teaspoon, dried)
> 1 teaspoon chopped chervil (½ teaspoon, dried)
> 2 cups fresh peas (or 1 package, frozen)
> 1 can tiny boiled onions
> 1 can tiny boiled potatoes
> Salt, pepper, paprika

Wash the chicken parts and put backs, necks, wing tips (save the wings for later), and giblets in a soup kettle with 3 quarts of water and 1 tablespoon of salt. Add the parsley and the onions, garlic, celery stalks, whole. Let this stock come to a boil and then simmer for 1½ hours. Drain the stock into another big kettle and cool the chicken enough to handle comfortably. Trim and cube the giblets, removing all gristle; strip bits of meat from the chicken necks and backs. Discard all bones and the whole vegetables.

Add to the chicken stock the barley, chopped celery, kidney beans, tomatoes, and spinach, along with the herbs and spices. Taste for salt and add more as needed. Simmer the soup for another hour, then add the giblets, chicken bits, and the wings dusted with paprika. Simmer for ½ hour, then toss in the peas, onions and potatoes (drained of juice), for a final 15 minutes of gentle boiling. Serve in big, shallow soup bowls and have a bone plate handy for the bones and skins of the wings. Makes about 6 quarts.

BASIL JELLY
FOR
ROAST LAMB

> 4 cups apple juice made from tart
> (greening) apples
> 2 tablespoons strained lemon juice
> 2 cups sugar
> 10 to 12 sprigs fresh basil

Boil up the juices and sugar, stirring until the sugar is dissolved. When well a-boil, throw in the basil sprigs. When the jelly stage is reached (when two drops "sheet" together when dripped from spoon), strain out the basil leaves and pour into scalded jelly glasses. When cool, tuck 3 or 4 basil leaves in each jar, then seal. Makes 4 to 6 small glassfuls.

STUFFING
FOR
CROWN ROAST
OF LAMB

> 4 cups soft fresh bread crumbs
> 1 stick butter, well softened
> ½ clove garlic, minced and mashed
> ¼ cup minced onion
> ½ cup finely chopped celery
> ¼ cup chopped parsley
> 1 teaspoon chopped fresh rosemary
> 1 teaspoon chopped fresh thyme
> 1 teaspoon salt
> ¼ teaspoon pepper

Crumble the fresh bread crumbs from time to time as they dry out a little, then work in the softened butter with the fingertips. Add the remaining ingredients and fork over lightly, so that all are well distributed. May be used also for roast stuffed leg or shoulder of lamb. Any stuffing not used may be frozen.

LAMB
AND
LEEK STEW

1½ pounds lamb chunks, lean and boneless
2 tablespoons olive oil
1 small onion, chopped
1 clove garlic, sliced thin
2 teaspoons salt
1 teaspoon peppercorns
1 bay leaf
2 cups raw cubed potatoes
2 cups leeks cut in 1-inch pieces
½ cup carrots, diced
1 cup green beans, broken small (or ½ package, frozen)
1 teaspoon chopped rosemary (½ teaspoon dried)

Brown the lamb in the olive oil, adding the onion and garlic as the lamb browns. Cover with boiling water and add the salt, peppercorns, and bay leaf. Cover the pot and let the lamb simmer gently for 1½ hours, or until nearly tender. Taste for salt; add more if needed. Add the remaining vegetables and the rosemary, and continue cooking until the vegetables are tender —about 30 minutes. Makes 4 to 6 servings.

STUFFED
CABBAGE

1 small white cabbage
1 cup sausage meat
1 cup ground veal
1 clove garlic, minced fine and mashed
2 tablespoons minced parsley
½ teaspoon marjoram
Salt and pepper
1 teaspoon flour
½ cup beef stock
2 small onions
2 carrots
2 slices salt pork or bacon

Submerge the head of cabbage in boiling water and parboil it for 5 minutes. Remove it from the pot and plunge it into cold water for 5 minutes. Drain well. The leaves may now be bent back to receive the stuffing. Prepare stuffing by mixing the meats thoroughly with the garlic, parsley, marjoram, ½ teaspoon of salt, and ¼ teaspoon of pepper. Fry this mixture for 5 minutes to draw off some of the sausage fat, then mix in the flour and 2 tablespoons of the stock.

Bury some of the stuffing in the heart of the cabbage and tuck spoonfuls in among the leaves, folding them back to lie as naturally as possible. When all stuffing has been used up, tie up the cabbage with string so that it will hold its shape.

Shred the onions and carrots, dice the salt pork or bacon, and lay these in the bottom of a casserole deep enough to hold the cabbage, covered. Add the remaining stock; sprinkle with salt and pepper. Lay the stuffed cabbage on this bed; cover the casserole and bake at 350° for 3 hours. Baste frequently with the stock and vegetables, and let the dish be uncovered for the last ½ hour to brown slightly. Before serving, remove the string. Cut the cabbage into wedges, like pie, and serve with the stock and its vegetables as dressing. Makes 6 to 8 servings.

ASPARAGUS
CASSEROLE

2 cups sliced mushrooms
1 tablespoon minced onion
2 tablespoons butter
4 tablespoons flour
1 cup chicken broth
1 cup milk
½ teaspoon salt
1 teaspoon Worcestershire sauce
24 stalks asparagus, cooked
2 hard-boiled eggs, sliced
½ cup coarse toasted bread crumbs

Sauté the mushrooms and onion in butter, then add the flour, chicken broth, and milk to make a cream sauce. Add the seasonings. Lay the cooked asparagus stalks in a casserole, top with the egg slices and pour on the sauce. Top with crumbs. Bake 20 to 30 minutes at 375°. Makes 4 servings.

LUNCHEON
ASPARAGUS
OR
BROCCOLI

4 squares toast
4 slices boiled or baked ham
24 stalks asparagus or 1 head broccoli
    cut in quarters lengthwise, cooked
2 cups cream sauce
2 cups grated sharp Cheddar cheese
1 teaspoon Worcestershire sauce
2 tablespoons chopped chives
Salt and pepper

The various ingredients may be prepared ahead of time but should not be chilled. To assemble the dish, spread the toast in an ovenproof platter, or put the slices in individual shallow casseroles. Lay a slice of ham on each square of toast, and on the ham arrange six stalks of asparagus, or an equivalent amount of broccoli; sprinkle lightly with salt and pepper (you may roll up the vegetables in the ham slices if you like). Blanket with the cream sauce into which the Cheddar cheese, Worcestershire sauce and chives have been stirred. Heat in a 300° oven for 20 minutes, then slip under the broiler for a few moments, until the cheese topping is flecked with brown. Makes 4 servings.

CALIFORNIA
GREEN BEANS*

4 cups young green beans, cross-cut in
  ½-inch pieces
2 cups celery, cut to match
3 tablespoons butter
½ teaspoon Lawry's seasoning salt

Boil the beans briskly in salted water for 10 to 15 minutes. Taste one at 10 minutes: the beans should be just barely tender, still crisp to the bite. Drain off the liquid and keep the beans hot in the pan. Meanwhile sauté the celery in the butter—again, taste for doneness at 8 minutes. The celery should brown a little but remain moist with butter. While it is sautéing, sprinkle on the seasoning salt. To serve, pour the beans on the celery and stir to absorb all the seasoned butter. Makes 4 to 6 servings.

GREEN BEANS
WITH HERBS

> 2½ cups green beans, French cut (or 1
> package frozen)
> 1 teaspoon chopped onion
> 1 teaspoon fresh dill or ½ teaspoon
> ground dill seed
> ½ teaspoon salt
> ⅔ cup sour cream

Cook beans, onion, and dill in ½ cup briskly boiling salted water for 15 minutes, until just tender. Most of the water should be absorbed. Add sour cream and heat, without boiling. Makes 4 small servings.

BEET GREENS

2 quarts beet thinnings or tops of young
   beets
3 strips bacon
1 tablespoon minced onion
2 tablespoons vinegar
½ teaspoon sugar
1 hard-cooked egg, sliced
Salt and pepper

Wash the greens thoroughly, discarding any yellowed leaves. Drain well. Fry the bacon until crisp, then remove it from the fat, crumble it, and keep it warm. In the bacon grease sauté the onion until it colors slightly, then add the greens, vinegar, and seasonings. Cook, covered, until the greens are just tender—6 to 10 minutes. Stir in the crumbled bacon and serve garnished with the egg slices. Depending upon the quantity of greens available, one must vary the amounts of the other ingredients. Tasting as you go along is the best guide. Makes about 4 servings.

BEETS
IN
ORANGE SAUCE

1 tablespoon butter
3 tablespoons brown sugar
1½ tablespoons flour
¾ cup orange juice
1 tablespoon grated orange rind
1 teaspoon grated lemon rind
¼ teaspoon salt
⅛ teaspoon paprika
2½ cups diced cooked beets

Melt the butter in a double boiler; add sugar mixed with flour and stir in the orange juice and seasonings. Cook until thick, stirring well. Add the beets and heat thoroughly. Makes 4 servings.

POLISH
BEETS*

2 cups cooked beets (about 12 small ones), grated or mashed fine with a fork
2 tablespoons sugar
½ teaspoon salt
¼ teaspoon fresh-ground pepper
2 tablespoons vinegar
1 tablespoon flour
½ cup sour cream

Put the beets in a saucepan; sprinkle them with the seasonings and vinegar. Sift in the flour, taking care that it doesn't lump. Heat this mixture thoroughly, then stir in the sour cream. Serve when piping hot, but never boiling. Makes 4 servings.

BROCCOLI
TIPS
ON
LETTUCE

2 tablespoons butter
Outside leaves of lettuce
2 cups small tips of broccoli
1 scallion or 1 tablespoon chopped chives
½ teaspoon salt

Put a thin slice of butter in the bottom of a heavy skillet large enough to take the broccoli tips in one layer. Line the skillet with dripping, just-washed outside leaves of lettuce. Spread the broccoli tips on the bed of lettuce. Sliver the scallion or chives on top, dust very lightly with salt, and dot with the remaining butter. Cover the broccoli with another lettuce leaf or two; cover the pan and set it over high heat just long enough to heat the pan thoroughly. When you can hear the butter bubble, lower the heat and let the broccoli simmer until just tender—about 10 minutes. Before serving, fish out the lettuce and pour any juice that remains upon the broccoli. Makes 4 servings.

RED CABBAGE
DE LUXE*

>   1 small red cabbage
>   1 small onion
>   1 big tart apple
>   1 teaspoon salt
>   ¼ teaspoon pepper
>   1 tablespoon butter
>   ½ cup dry red wine
>   ¼ cup grape jelly

Slice the cabbage and onion thin; pare, quarter, and core the apple. Set all these to cook in 1 cup of boiling water, seasoning with the salt and pepper. Add the butter and wine. Cover the pot and let the cabbage cook briskly for 30 minutes. Add the grape jelly and continue cooking for another 10 minutes. If all juice is not absorbed, thicken with a teaspoon or two of flour. Makes 4 to 6 servings.

FLEMISH
CARROTS*

4 cups raw carrots (about 12 small
ones), cut julienne
3 tablespoons butter
½ teaspoon sugar
½ teaspoon salt
1 tablespoon minced parsley

OPTIONAL   1 teaspoon flour
½ cup light cream

The carrots should be cut julienne, in thin strips, lengthwise.
Put them in a saucepan with all the other ingredients (except
the optional flour and cream). Add 2 tablespoons of water;
cover the pan and let the carrots cook briskly until tender—7
minutes, no more. Drain off any butter that is not absorbed in
the cooking. If desired, cream blended with flour may be added
to make creamed carrots. Makes 4 servings.

CARROTS
FRANÇOISE

6–8 carrots, sliced
1 medium-sized onion
1 tablespoon butter
½ teaspoon salt
2 tablespoons chopped parsley

Parboil the carrots in salted water for 8 minutes, then drain. Shred the onion and brown it in the butter. Add the carrots and heat well. Stir in the parsley just before serving. Makes 4 servings.

HUNGARIAN
CARROTS

4 cups raw carrots, cut julienne
2 tablespoons butter
2 tablespoons flour
½ teaspoon salt
½ cup orange juice
1 tablespoon grated orange peel
1 tablespoon grated lemon peel
3 tablespoons brown sugar

The carrots should be cut julienne, in thin strips, lengthwise. Melt the butter, add the carrots and sauté them lightly for 5 minutes. Sprinkle on the flour and salt, then add the orange juice, the peel, sugar, and 1 cup of water. Simmer gently for about 20 minutes, until the carrots are tender. Makes 4 servings.

CORN-TOMATO
CASSEROLE*

3 cups raw corn cut from cob
6 tomatoes, sliced thick
½ onion, chopped fine
1 green pepper, chopped fine
Salt and pepper
2 tablespoons butter
1 cup coarse fresh bread crumbs, well
   dried
3 slices bacon, diced

Spread half the corn in a buttered casserole, cover it with slices of tomato laid close together. Sprinkle on half the onion and green pepper, dust with salt and pepper, and dot with half the butter. Add another layer in the same order. Top the casserole with the bread crumbs and diced bacon. Bake at 375° for 45 minutes. Makes 4 servings.

FRIED CORN

4 slices bacon
1 small onion, chopped
½ green pepper, chopped
2 cups cooked corn
Salt and pepper

Fry the bacon crisp. Lift it from the fat, crumble it, and keep it warm. Drain off all but 3 tablespoons of the bacon fat, and in this sauté the onion and green pepper, letting them brown lightly. Turn in the corn; sprinkle with pepper and add salt if needed. Stir the corn around to absorb the fat and then cook gently for 5 minutes, until the corn is thoroughly heated. Just before serving, mix in the crumbled bacon. Makes 4 servings.

CORN PANCAKES

6 ears corn, grated raw
3 eggs, beaten separately
½ teaspoon salt
⅓ to ½ cup butter

The corn should be scraped or grated so that the kernel skins are discarded. Add the corn and salt to the well-beaten egg yolks, then fold in the whipped egg whites. Drop by spoonfuls into bubbling butter. When the pancakes are turned, they will puff up like baby soufflés and are meltingly tender. Since they fall quickly, this is a dish best prepared at the table. Makes 18 to 24 small pancakes.

ROASTING
EARS

> Ears of corn with husks on
> Butter
> Salt

Pick the corn in the morning and put it at once in cold water. Pull the husks open just enough to remove the worst of the silk, then refold the husks in place. Let the corn stand in a bucket of water until roasting time. When the fire in the terrace grill is glowing coals, lay ears on the grill and roast for 18 to 20 minutes, turning frequently so that the husks do not burn through and scorch the kernels. Have at hand a shaker of salt and a bowl of melted butter with a pastry brush. When the corn is roasted, pull the husks all the way back (they will cool quickly and may be used as a handle), paint the ears with butter, and sprinkle them with salt.

EGGPLANT
CASSEROLE*

1 clove garlic, minced

2 tablespoons minced onion

2 tablespoons olive oil

2 cups cooked lamb, cubed

1 medium-sized eggplant, pared and cubed (3 cups)

2 cups tomatoes, peeled and cut up

2 tablespoons chopped parsley

½ teaspoon fresh marjoram

½ teaspoon fresh thyme

1 teaspoon salt

¼ teaspoon pepper

4 ripe olives, sliced

½ cup coarse bread crumbs, well dried

2 tablespoons grated Parmesan or Romano cheese

Sauté the garlic and onion in the olive oil for 5 minutes, then add the lamb and let it brown. Add the eggplant, stirring it around to absorb flavor, then add ¼ cup of water, the tomatoes, parsley, seasonings, and sliced olives. Turn all into a casserole, top with the crumbs mixed with the cheese, and bake at 400° for 15 minutes. If the crumb topping has not browned sufficiently, slip the casserole under the broiler for a moment before serving. Makes 4 servings.

BAKED
SLICED
EGGPLANT

1 medium-sized eggplant
¼ to ½ cup softened butter
Salt
Paprika
2 tablespoons chopped parsley
2 tablespoons chopped chives
Slices of lemon

Pare the eggplant and cut it in slices one half inch thick. Spread one side generously with very soft butter, dust lightly with salt and paprika, then lay the slices butter side down on a cookie sheet. Now butter and dust the top sides with salt and paprika. Bake at 400° for 15 to 20 minutes, until the eggplant is tender and crisply brown. Turn the slices once. Garnish with the parsley, chives, and lemon slices. Makes 4 servings.

POTPOURRI
OF KALE*

4 large link sausages
4 to 6 large onions
1½ pounds kale
4 large tomatoes
4 to 6 okra pods
1 teaspoon salt
Fresh ground pepper

Simmer the sausages in water for 5 mintues while you peel the onions and wash and dry the kale. Cut off the stems and any tough midriffs. Prick the sausages in several places and put them in a large deep skillet to brown. As fat accumulates, slice the onions into it and fry until the sausages begin to brown and the onions are transparent. Cut in the tomatoes and okra—stem ends removed—in chunks. Add the kale, as much as the skillet will hold. Cook briskly, stirring frequently so that the liquid will be absorbed, until the kale is just tender but not limp—say 15 minutes. The curly leaves should stand up in the pot. Just before serving, add a teaspoon of salt and grind fresh pepper generously on top. Makes 4 generous servings.

BRAISED
LEEKS

½ small onion
1 tablespoon butter
2 cups chicken stock
½ bay leaf
1 whole clove
3 to 4 peppercorns
1 teaspoon salt, if needed
3 to 5 leeks per person, depending on
   thickness
1 tablespoon flour
Squares of toast

Slice the onion into a heavy skillet and brown it lightly in the butter, then add the stock and seasonings. Let this boil up. Add the leeks, trimmed of roots and tops, and cook uncovered until the leeks are tender (thumb-sized leeks take about 15 minutes) and the sauce much reduced. Keep the leeks hot while you strain the liquid and thicken it with 1 tablespoon of flour to 1 cup of liquid. Serve the leeks on toast, with the sauce poured over them. Directions for the sauce are predicated on 4 servings.

PISELLI
ALL' ITALIANO*

1 tablespoon minced parsley
1 small whole onion
1 sliver garlic
1 tablespoon olive oil
3 thin slices boiled ham
4 cups peas (and a few pods)
½ teaspoon salt
1 tablespoon butter

Sauté the parsley, onion, and garlic in the olive oil for 2 minutes. Add the ham, chopped fine, fat and lean together. Cook until the ham shrinks, about 5 minutes. Remove the garlic and add the peas, stirring them well to absorb the oily sauce. Add 2 tablespoons of water, the salt and butter. Throw in a few pods for flavor. Cover the pan and let the peas simmer until tender —15 to 20 minutes. If all the juice does not absorb in the cooking, thicken it with a little sifted flour. Before serving, remove onion and pods. Makes 4 servings.

TOMATOES
BAKED
WITH HERBS

4 large well-rounded tomatoes
Salt and pepper
1 tablespoon onion, minced fine
2 tablespoons chopped fresh basil
2 tablespoons chopped fresh dill
1 teaspoon celery seed
½ cup coarse bread crumbs, dried
4 teaspoons butter

Remove the stem ends from the tomatoes without cutting into the flesh. Cut the tomatoes in half; do not peel them. Place them cut side up in a shallow baking dish or casserole. Sprinkle with salt and pepper, onion, and herbs. Give the tomatoes a topping of bread crumbs; dot with butter. Bake at 400° for about 15 minutes. Makes 4 servings.

FRIED
GREEN
TOMATOES

Green tomatoes
Flour
Salt
Butter

Select hard green tomatoes, preferably touched by frost. Slice them one half inch thick, discarding a thin slice at blossom and stem ends. Dip the slices in salted flour, then fry in a generous amount of butter. They should fry crisp and dark brown, almost to the point of charring—5 minutes a side should be enough. Add more butter as you turn the slices if the pan is dry.

BAKED
STUFFED
ZUCCHINI

4 zucchini, about 6 inches long
⅓ cup fresh bread crumbs
1 teaspoon minced onion
Slice of garlic, minced
¼ cup chopped cooked mushrooms
½ teaspoon salt
¼ teaspoon fresh ground pepper
¼ teaspoon dried orégano
⅔ cup sour cream
¼ cup toasted bread crumbs
2 tablespoons butter

Parboil the zucchini, halved lengthwise, in boiling salted water for 2 minutes, then drain and scoop out the soft centers. Mix this pulp lightly with the fresh bread crumbs, onion, garlic, mushrooms, seasonings, and sour cream. Pile this mixture in the zucchini boats. Sprinkle toasted bread crumbs on top, dot with butter, and bake for 20 minutes at 350°. Makes 4 servings.

STEWED
ZUCCHINI

Slice of garlic, minced and crushed
2 tablespoons olive oil
6 small zucchini, 4 to 6 inches long
½ teaspoon salt
1 tablespoon chopped parsley
1 teaspoon minced chives
Fresh ground pepper

Sauté the garlic in olive oil, then add the zucchini sliced about
one half inch thick. Roll the zucchini around in the oil so that
they are thoroughly coated. Add the salt and 1 tablespoon of
water; cover the pan tightly and let simmer for 3 to 5 minutes,
until the zucchini are tender but not mushy. Just before serving, stir in the parsley and chives and give the dish a grating
of fresh pepper. Makes 4 servings.

RATATOUILLE

1 medium eggplant
5 tomatoes
3 zucchini
4 green peppers
1 onion
1 clove garlic
½ cup olive oil
1 teaspoon salt
1 bay leaf
½ teaspoon fresh chopped thyme
½ teaspoon fresh ground pepper
Dash of red pepper

Pare the eggplant, slice it 1½ inches thick, and quarter the slices. Remove stem ends from tomatoes; quarter them. Slice the zucchini 1 inch thick; seed the green peppers and cut them in 1-inch squares. Quarter the onion and slice the garlic. Put all the vegetables in a heavy saucepan and add the oil and seasonings. Cover the pot and simmer for 30 minutes, stirring occasionally, but carefully, to avoid breaking the vegetables. If the mixture is too liquid for a good stew, remove the cover and cook until the sauce is reduced. Do not let the vegetables overcook. Makes 6 to 8 servings.

VEGETABLE
CASSEROLE I

1 cup green beans, cut in 1-inch pieces
1 cup carrots, sliced ¼ inch thick
1 cup raw potatoes, cut in ½-inch cubes
½ cup sliced celery
½ cup sliced scallions
½ cup sliced leeks (optional)
½ cup green pepper, cut in 1-inch
squares
2 tablespoons butter
2 8-ounce cans tomato sauce
½ teaspoon salt
¼ teaspoon pepper
1 teaspoon chopped fresh basil

Simmer the beans, carrots, potatoes, and celery in 1 inch of boiling water for 10 minutes. Meanwhile sauté the scallions, leeks, and green pepper in the butter. When they are tender, add the tomato sauce and seasonings. When the sauce is hot, drain the vegetables and pour the sauce over them. Cook, covered, over low heat for 10 minutes, or until the vegetables are tender. Makes 8 servings.

VEGETABLE
CASSEROLE II

1 cup thin-sliced leeks
1 cup thin-sliced celery
1 cup chopped green pepper
2 teaspoons minced onion
2 tablespoons butter
2 cups fresh peas
1½ teaspoons salt
¼ teaspoon fresh-ground pepper
2 tablespoons chopped basil
3 tablespoons heavy cream

Sauté the leeks, celery, green pepper, and onion in the butter for 5 minutes. Add the peas, seasonings, and 2 tablespoons boiling water. Cover and cook over low heat until the peas are tender—about 12 minutes. Before serving, add the cream. Heat, but do not allow to boil. Makes 4 servings.

TOSSED
SALAD
WITH HERBS

1 clove garlic
Lettuce of various varieties, equivalent
   of 2 to 3 quarts
2 to 3 scallions
¼ teaspoon fresh-ground pepper
1 teaspoon minced chervil
1 teaspoon minced tarragon
3 tablespoons olive oil
1 tablespoon lemon juice
½ teaspoon salt (to start)

Cut the garlic in half and rub a large wooden bowl vigorously
with the cut halves, crushing the garlic to release its oils and
juices. Discard the garlic. Break into the bowl well-washed and
dried lettuce, turning it over and over very lightly to come in
contact with the film of garlic. Slice the scallions on the lettuce,
and scatter the herbs and pepper on top. Measure the oil into
a big wooden spoon and sprinkle it on the salad; then measure
into the spoon the lemon juice and salt, stirring until the salt
is dissolved. Sprinkle this on the salad and start tossing lightly,
turning the lettuce gently until every leaf is coated and the
seasonings are well distributed. Taste for salt before serving:
it may need up to a teaspoon, depending upon the quantity of
lettuce. Makes 4 servings.

Other herb combinations for tossed salad: dill and basil;
summer savory and thyme; chives, chervil, and basil.

BOHEMIAN
BEET SALAD
WITH
ANCHOVIES

1 large bunch watercress
½ cucumber
½ small Chinese cabbage
4 hard-cooked eggs
6 to 8 small beets, boiled
1 tablespoon chopped chives
½ teaspoon fresh chopped marjoram
6 anchovy fillets, chopped small
Spiced salad dressing

Line a shallow bowl with watercress, and upon it intermingle slices of cucumber with cross-cut slices of Chinese cabbage. Arrange slices of the eggs and beets on top of this. Sprinkle with the herbs and anchovies. When ready to serve at table, pour on spiced salad dressing and toss well. Makes 6 servings.

BELGIAN TOMATOES*

1 large Spanish onion
4 well-ripened tomatoes
¼ teaspoon sugar
½ teaspoon salt
Fresh-ground pepper
2 tablespoons chopped fresh chives
2 tablespoons chopped fresh basil
2 tablespoons chopped fresh dill
1 teaspoon celery seed

OPTIONAL

Oil and vinegar

This dish should be prepared on the platter from which it will be served. Slice the onion in thin rings; separate the rings and spread them over the bottom of the platter. Dispose thickish slices of peeled tomatoes on the onion. Dust them with the sugar, salt, and pepper; sprinkle on the herbs. Cover the platter with foil and chill until serving time. You may give it a sprinkling of oil and vinegar if you wish. Makes 4 to 6 servings.

CAESAR
SALAD*

2 heads of Romaine or Great Lakes lettuce
1 clove garlic
6 anchovy fillets
3 tablespoons grated Parmesan cheese
1 egg
3 tablespoons olive oil
1 tablespoon red wine vinegar
1 cup croutons
2 tablespoons melted butter

Have the lettuce well washed, thoroughly dried, and chilled. Make the dressing (it can be done well ahead of time) as follows: Mash the garlic in a large wooden bowl, rubbing it well around the sides. Put in the anchovy fillets and cheese and mash them to a paste. Boil the egg 1 minute—the white should be slightly coddled—and add it to the paste, blending well. Work it all smooth with the oil and vinegar. Prepare the croutons by tossing them in the melted butter, then drying them to a brown crisp in the oven.

To serve, break the lettuce into the salad bowl, add the croutons, and toss until each leaf is well coated and the croutons have absorbed some of the dressing. Makes 4 servings.

SALAD
NIÇOISE

6 small firm tomatoes, peeled and quar-
   tered
1 green pepper, cut in thin strips
2 small onions, cut in thin rings
½ cup coarsely chopped celery
½ cup Italian black olives (the
   shrunken variety), sliced
6 fillets of anchovy, cut small
¼ cup French dressing made with wine
   vinegar

Have all ingredients thoroughly chilled. Arrange them in a
shallow bowl with an eye for color contrasts. Mix lightly with
the dressing. Serve with French bread and sweet butter. Makes
4 servings.

SOUR-CREAM
CUCUMBERS*

1 scant tablespoon sugar
½ teaspoon salt
2 tablespoons cider vinegar
1 cup sour cream
2 tablespoons chopped chives
2 tablespoons chopped fresh dill, head
  and leaves
1 teaspoon celery seed
2 cucumbers

Dissolve sugar and salt in the vinegar, then stir in the sour cream. Add the seasonings. Slice the cucumbers very thin, rind and all, and mix them thoroughly into the dressing, seeing to it that every slice is coated. Chill for several hours before serving. Makes 4 servings.

GARLIC
DRESSING

6 garlic cloves, crushed to a paste
1 teaspoon salt
Juice of 2 lemons
Olive oil

Combine the first three ingredients and add an equal quantity of olive oil. Store in a screw-top jar, and shake and strain before using. The flavor improves with keeping. Use as a dressing with tossed greens. Good also on stewed zucchini. Makes about 1 cup.

SPICED
SALAD
DRESSING

2 cups olive oil
½ cup red wine vinegar
2 teaspoons sugar
1 teaspoon salt
¼ teaspoon pepper
2 tablespoons tomato sauce
2 tablespoons chili sauce
½ teaspoon orégano
⅛ teaspoon cayenne pepper
½ green pepper, seeded
2 slices onion
½ clove garlic

Put all these ingredients into a blender and whirl for 1 minute, or until all ingredients are mingled. Stored in a screw-top jar, this dressing will keep well in the refrigerator and may be used as needed. Makes 1½ pints.

BASIL
VINEGAR

> Leaves of basil to fill a pint jar ¾ full
> Red wine vinegar to fill the jar

Pack basil leaves in a heated, screw-top jar, crushing them slightly to release the aromatic oils. Heat the vinegar to boiling and pour it over the basil leaves. Screw the cover on tightly and let the vinegar steep for 2 weeks. Strain out the leaves and bottle the vinegar.

TARRAGON
VINEGAR

> Tarragon sprigs to fill a pint jar ¾ full
> White wine vinegar to fill the jar

Procedure is the same as for Basil Vinegar.

RHUBARB SAUCE WITH RASPBERRIES

> 4 cups rhubarb, cut in 1-inch pieces
> ½ cup sugar
> 2 teaspoons grated lemon rind
> ¼ teaspoon cinnamon
> 1 cup or more of ripe raspberries

Sprinkle the rhubarb with the sugar and let stand for an hour. Add the lemon rind and cinnamon; cook gently over low heat until the rhubarb is tender—about 10 minutes. Chill the sauce. Before serving, sprinkle the raspberries on top. They may be stirred gently into the sauce while it is hot, but will tend to disintegrate. Makes 4 servings.

DEEP-DISH
RHUBARB
AND
STRAWBERRY
PIE*

2½ cups fresh, diced rhubarb
¾ cup granulated sugar
2½ tablespoons minute tapioca
½ teaspoon lemon juice
1 teaspoon lemon rind, grated
⅛ teaspoon nutmeg
⅛ teaspoon salt
2 cups ripe strawberries
1 tablespoon butter
Pastry dough

Combine the rhubarb, sugar, tapioca, lemon juice and rind, nutmeg, and salt. Let stand for 15 minutes. Add the strawberries, hulled, washed, and drained. Pile all in a buttered baking dish and dot with the butter. Roll pastry dough ¼ inch thick and lay it on top, pinching the edges over the lip of the dish. Slash the crust in a V design. Bake for 10 minutes at 425°, then for 30 minutes at 350°. Makes 4 to 6 servings.

BAKED RHUBARB PUDDING

1 cup zwieback crumbs
3 cups diced raw rhubarb
1 teaspoon grated lemon peel
1 tablespoon grated orange peel
½ cup sugar
2 tablespoons butter

Butter a baking dish. Sprinkle half the crumbs in the bottom and cover with the rhubarb combined with the lemon and orange peel and the sugar. Top with the remaining crumbs and dot with butter. Bake at 350° until rhubarb is tender and the crumb topping brown—20 to 25 minutes. Makes 4 servings.

STRAWBERRIES WITH BRANDY

1 quart ripe strawberries
¼ cup strained honey
¼ to ⅓ cup brandy
Sour cream

Hull and wash the berries; let them dry on paper towels. Put them in a bowl and dribble honey and brandy over them. Roll the berries around very gently to give them a thorough coating of the liquid. Chill for at least 2 hours, once or twice stirring the top berries under so that all may soak in the sauce. Pass a bowl of sour cream with the strawberries. Or you may wish to use them as a sauce for French vanilla ice cream or pineapple ice. Makes 4 servings.

21

SOME SUGGESTIONS
FOR THE
GOURMET GARDENER'S
BOOKSHELF

Burrage on Vegetables, Albert C. Burrage. D. Van Nostrand Co., Inc., New York, 1954

Food Garden, The, Laurence and Edna Blair. The Macmillan Co., New York, 1945

Fruits for the Home Garden, U. P. Hedrick. Oxford University Press, New York, 1944

253

Garden Spice and Wild Pot Herbs, Muenscher and Rice. Cornell University Press, Ithaca, N.Y., 1955

Gardener's Bug Book, The, Cynthia Westcott. American Garden Guild and Doubleday & Co., New York, 1956

Gardening for Good Eating, Helen Morgenthau Fox. The Macmillan Co., New York, 1943

Gardening Indoors Under Lights, Frederick and Jacqueline Kranz, Viking Press, New York, 1957

Grow Your Own Vegetables, Paul V. Dempsey. Houghton Mifflin Co., Boston, Mass., 1944

Growing Plants Under Artificial Light, Peggie Schulz. M. Barrows & Co., Inc., New York, 1955

Herbs, How to Grow Them and How to Use Them, Helen N. Webster. Charles T. Branford Co., Boston, Mass., 1952

Herbs, Their Culture and Uses, Rosetta E. Clarkson. The Macmillan Co., New York, 1954

Practical Gardening, Olive Mason Gunnison. American Garden Guild and Doubleday & Co., New York, 1955

Vegetables for Your Home Garden, John H. Melady. Grosset & Dunlap, New York, 1952

Vegetable Gardening for Everyone, L. Richard Guylay. World Publishing Co., Cleveland, Ohio, 1944

___MAGAZINES

Horticulture (monthly) Horticultural Hall, Boston, Mass.

Plants and Gardens (quarterly) Brooklyn Botanic Garden, Brooklyn, N.Y.

Popular Gardening (monthly) Gardening Publications, Inc., Albany, N.Y.

INDEX

255

Index

213, 232, 239, 240
Braised, 232
culture of, 54, 57, 64, 65, 73, 140,
183
fall care of, 140
in recipes, 210, 213, 232, 239, 240
to clean, 141
to freeze, 141–42
lettuce, 22, 23, 28, 32–33, 37, 54, 56,
58, 64, 65, 68, 69, 70, 72, 73, 86,
98, 99, 100, 102, 103, 104, 105,
108, 110, 118, 136, 184, 190,
191, 194, 197, 241, 244
culture of, 54, 56, 58, 64, 65, 69,
73, 99–100, 102, 103, 184
grown under lights, 190, 191, 192,
194, 197
in salad, 241, 244
romaine, 33, 184, 244
varieties of, 32–33, 37, 184
lime (*see also* fertilizing; soil), 49,
61–62, 155
and peat moss, 155
limestone, ground, 49, 52, 122
loam. See soil
log, garden (*see also* jottings), 35,
43–44, 107–10
Luncheon Asparagus or Broccoli, 216

manure, 44–45, 48, 52, 59, 121, 122,
132, 155, 156, 164, 167, 170
marjoram (*see also* herbs), 32, 37,
146, 148, 149, 181, 190, 194,
195, 198, 206, 208, 214, 229,
242
as house plant, 146
grown under lights, 190, 194, 195,
196, 197
in recipes, 206, 208, 214, 229, 242
menu suggestions, 20, 44, 63, 123,
136, 137, 139
Minestra, 206
mint, 23, 112, 182
mulching, 76–77, 96, 117, 121, 140,
149–50, 152, 171

herbs, 149–50, 152
leeks, 140
materials, 76, 77, 140, 149

octopus, the, 82-83
okra, 33, 111, 184, 231
Onion Soup, French, 207
onions, 23, 29, 30, 37, 54, 57, 64, 65,
70, 73, 86, 110, 111, 132, 136,
137, 185, 203, 207, 208, 209,
231
culture of, 30, 54, 57, 64, 65, 70,
73, 185
from seed, 110
in recipes, 203, 207, 208, 209, 231
thinning of, 30, 70, 73

parsley, 32, 37, 54, 64, 71, 74, 146,
150, 151, 182, 190, 194
as house plant, 146, 151
culture of, 54, 64, 71, 74, 150–51,
182
grown under lights, 190, 194
paths, garden, 142–43, 158
peas, 23, 34, 37, 42, 46, 47–48, 54,
57, 58, 60, 63, 64, 65, 70, 74,
85, 86, 110, 118, 135, 185, 206,
208, 233, 240
culture of, 42, 54, 57, 58, 64, 65,
70, 74, 185
in Piselli All' Italiano, 60, 233
in recipes, 206, 208, 233, 240
interplanting, 34
supports for, 46, 47–48, 63–64
varieties of, 34, 37
peat moss (*see also* soil preparation),
44, 49, 52, 77, 122, 132, 155,
167
and lime, 155
peppers, green, 23, 33, 38, 55, 58, 64,
65, 70, 87, 137, 143, 185–86,
198, 202, 226, 227, 238, 239,
240, 245, 247
culture of, 55, 58, 64, 65, 137, 185

sand. *See* soil preparation
scallions (*see also* onions), 22, 23, 30,
    69, 70, 73, 86, 98, 110, 239,
    241
seed (s), 24, 36–37, 46, 54–57, 58,
    62, 65, 69, 102, 103, 195
    growing media for, 46, 55, 62, 195
    planting tricks, 55–57, 62, 102, 103
    order, 36–37
    spacing and depth, 58, 65
slugs. *See* pests
soil, 42, 43, 51, 52, 53, 56, 57, 61,
    62, 66, 76, 103, 117, 120, 121,
    155, 166, 167, 195
    conditioner, krilium, 53, 56, 66,
        103
    conditioning, 56, 61, 62, 66, 76, 103
    drainage, 53
    maintenance, 52, 76, 166, 167
    preparation, 51–53, 117, 120–21,
        155, 195
    test, 61
    workability of, 42, 43, 51
soup, 83–84, 203–10
    Cold Broccoli, 204
    Corn-Curry, 205
    French Onion, 207
    Hungarian Chicken-Pot, 208
    Minestra, 206
    Russian Bortsch, 203
    Vichyssoise, 210
Sour-Cream Cucumbers, 246
sphagnum moss, 62, 195
Spiced Salad Dressing, 247
Spiced Tomato Juice, 202
spinach 98, 99, 110, 206, 208
    New Zealand, 99
spraying. *See* pest control
spring planting, 39, 53–66, 67
squash, 23, 33, 34, 38, 48, 53, 55,
    58, 64, 66, 70, 86, 87, 89–90,
    101, 103, 111, 118, 136, 137,
    186, 198, 236, 237, 238
    butternut, 23
    culture of, 55, 64, 66, 186

fruiting of, 89–90
    zucchini, 33–34, 38, 58, 64, 66,
        87, 88, 89, 111, 136, 186, 198,
        236, 237, 238
stakes, 46, 48, 91, 92, 166, 169, 170,
    171
stepping stones, 142–43
Stewed Zucchini, 237
strawberries, 20, 21, 23, 110, 115,
    116–18, 120, 125, 126, 153, 250,
    252
    culture of, 116–18, 126
    with Brandy, 252
Strawberry Pie, Rhubarb and, 250
Stuffed Cabbage, 214
Stuffing for Crown Roast of Lamb,
    20, 212
succession sowing, 28, 40–41, 54, 95,
    97–102, 120, 127
summer care of garden, 75–84, 85–92,
    97–106
summer planting, 38, 98–102, 105–6
summer savory, 152, 182, 241
    in recipes, 152, 241
superphosphate, 44, 49, 52
supplies, garden, 44–49, 168
supports (*see also* stakes), 46, 47–48,
    60, 61, 63, 91, 92
    of coat hangers, 60, 61
    for peas, 46, 47–48, 63
    for tomatoes, 46, 48, 91, 92

tarragon, 32, 147, 148, 149, 150, 151,
    183, 241, 248
    in recipes, 241, 248
    Vinegar, 147, 151, 248
    wintering over, 148–49
thinning the garden (*see also* under
    vegetables by name), 55, 56, 69–
    72, 73, 86, 156
    with scissors, 71
thinnings, use of, 56, 69, 70, 72, 73,
    86
thyme (*see also* herbs), 32, 37, 146,
    148, 149, 150, 151, 183, 190,

261